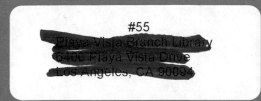

JOHN MUIR
NATURE'S VISIONARY

JOHN MUIR
NATURE'S VISIONARY

BY GRETEL EHRLICH

NATIONAL
GEOGRAPHIC

WASHINGTON, D.C.

Bathed in perpetual twilight, ferns thrive at the base of coastal redwoods in California's Muir Woods National Monument. "The best tree-lover's monument that could be found in all the forests of the world," Muir called it.

Preceding pages: Storm clouds billow above an osprey guarding its nest along the Suwannee River in Florida.

Page 1: Redwoods catch the California sunlight.

CONTENTS

Despite his love of adventure, Muir also relished his quiet times with nature, his contemplations in the "Godful solitude" of the Sierra Nevada and other wildernesses.

I Only Went Out for a Walk

T HE EARTH WAS ONCE ALL WILD. Mountain lakes were "young eyes opening to light." The snouts of glaciers shoveled granite aside, laying open valleys and stacking debris into vertical walls. The rough, irregular peaks pierced the air until sprays of transparent eyes tumbled, each one "a small world," "an unbroken ocean," and the days were embroidered by the solitary water ouzel's stream songs. In winter, whorled snowflowers drifted slowly down from "the dark, frozen sky," and the trees' columnar majesty was a grove under which human animals ate other living beings and were eaten. Fitness was an intelligence that allowed animals to know each other without words, and survival of the fittest was a kind of keenness that in no way could be used as a model for machined efficiency. In this world, beauty was the gross national product, and divinity was self-existing and resided in all things.

John Muir did not live the tragedy of sin and redemption in which he had been raised, because nature became his god and it was in him. He just lived;

he lowered himself down into glaciers and hoisted himself onto toppling peaks, so that he could speak from the point of view of ice, rock, cloud, and air, instead of from a self-cherishing human ego. His body was the instrument with which he measured, assessed, felt, and interpreted the elements, and in turn, he allowed nature to use him any way that it pleased.

He traveled light and often walked with no particular destination, because each inch of the path held answers and questions, the first step as rich as the last. The world came up through the soles of his feet and permeated his skin, nose, eyes, and ears, sparking the strings of intelligent cells and proteins there. He ate sequoia sap and let storm pulses shudder through his limbs as he clung to bucking, undulating trees. He was rained on, hailed on, snowed on, he fell and climbed and fell again and knew firsthand the dry mercilessness of nature. Yet, the more it tore into him, the more succulence he found; the more he surrendered to the natural world, the more wide awake he became.

He was not a passive observer in the mountains but a rambler and a questioner, an Emersonian eye—whole, transparent, curious. Rolling over the surface of the Earth, he slowly developed an ability to transform his physicality into verbal nimbleness once he came to town. There, he took on the role of a wildman, as if he had been raised by wolves instead of by his puritanical, evangelizing father. He walked the streets of San Francisco disheveled, long-haired, always lost in the confines of buildings, traffic, and pavement, and forever late. After all, truancy had been his curriculum during all of those years in the mountains; any intimacy requires unmeasured time.

No matter how many times Muir sauntered through Tuolumne Meadows, crossed Alaska's frozen lands, or wove between fruit trees in his home orchard, he still liked to put his head between his knees and look at the world upside down to remind himself of its newness, its "upness," its originality. He could always hear in the pine wind its "grand, smooth song." In the mountains of California and Alaska, the terrors of the human heart were unlocked and soothed by the deeper ones of the wild—the crumbling massifs of ice, the abysses of granite canyons, the wild tumult of mountain streams at high water changing courses in the night.

If open-heart surgery had been performed on John Muir, a mountain stippled with glaciers might have been found where the heart should have been and, tipped another way, could have served as an altar. In his late, undated journal fragments, he wrote: "Not like my taking the veil—no solemn abjuration of the world. I only went out for a walk, and finally concluded to stay out till sundown, for going out, I found, was really going in." ▪

JOHN MUIR: NATURE'S VISIONARY

I often wonder what man will do with the mountains. . . . will human destructions like those of Nature—fire and flood and avalanche— work out a higher good, a finer beauty?

~JM

Black oaks and ponderosa pines stand guard along the Merced River at the foot of Yosemite's El Capitan.

Following pages: Lupines blanket a meadow in the Mount Rainier backcountry, where Muir roamed on an 1888 trip through the Pacific Northwest.

T ake a course in good
water and air, and in the
eternal youth of Nature
you may renew your
own. Go quietly, alone;
no harm will befall you.

~JM

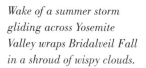

*Wake of a summer storm
gliding across Yosemite
Valley wraps Bridalveil Fall
in a shroud of wispy clouds.*

*Following pages: Muir did
not discover the wonders of
Arizona's Grand Canyon
until his later years, but he
became an ardent advocate
of protected status for the
canyon—a goal achieved
in 1908, when it was desig-
nated a national monument.*

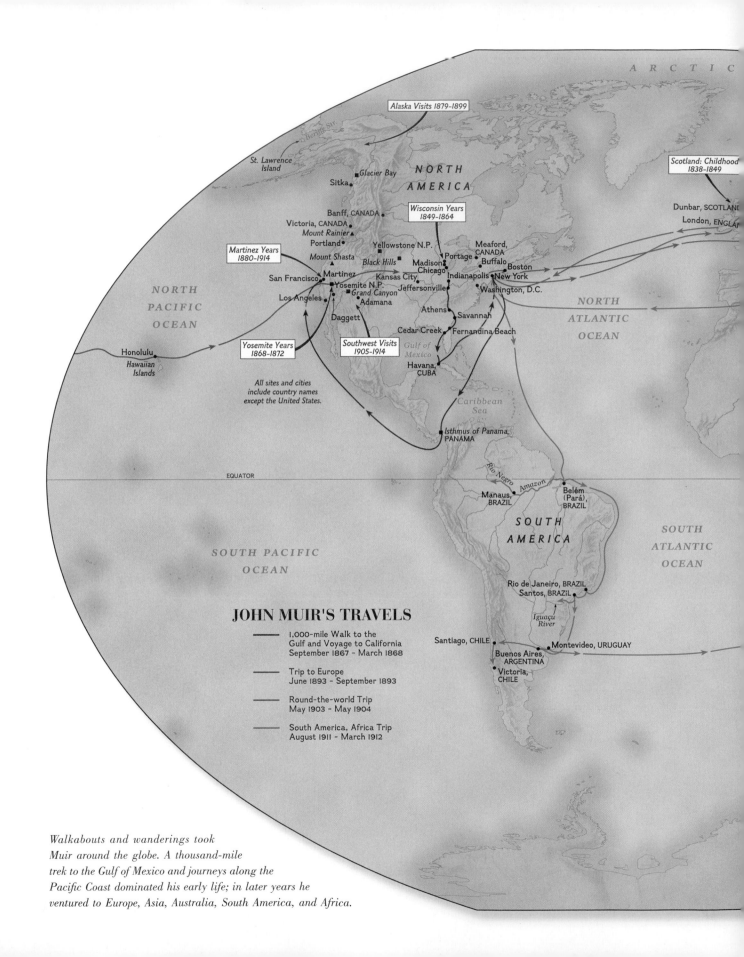

JOHN MUIR'S TRAVELS

— 1,000-mile Walk to the
    Gulf and Voyage to California
    September 1867 – March 1868

— Trip to Europe
    June 1893 – September 1893

— Round-the-world Trip
    May 1903 – May 1904

— South America, Africa Trip
    August 1911 – March 1912

Alaska Visits 1879–1899

Scotland: Childhood 1838–1849

NORTH
AMERICA

Wisconsin Years 1849–1864

Dunbar, SCOTLAND
London, ENGLAND

Martinez Years 1880–1914

Meaford, CANADA

St. Lawrence Island

Glacier Bay

Sitka

Banff, CANADA
Victoria, CANADA
Mount Rainier
Portland
Mount Shasta
Black Hills
Yellowstone N.P.
Madison
Chicago
Portage
Buffalo
Boston
San Francisco
Martinez
Kansas City
Indianapolis
New York
Yosemite N.P.
Jeffersonville
Washington, D.C.
Los Angeles
Grand Canyon
Adamana
Athens
Daggett
Cedar Creek
Savannah
Fernandina Beach

NORTH
PACIFIC
OCEAN

NORTH
ATLANTIC
OCEAN

Honolulu
Hawaiian Islands

Yosemite Years 1868–1872

Southwest Visits 1905–1914

Gulf of Mexico

Havana, CUBA

*All sites and cities
include country names
except the United States.*

Caribbean Sea

EQUATOR

Isthmus of Panama, PANAMA

Rio Negro
Amazon
Manaus, BRAZIL
Belém (Pará), BRAZIL

SOUTH
AMERICA

SOUTH
ATLANTIC
OCEAN

SOUTH PACIFIC
OCEAN

Rio de Janeiro, BRAZIL
Santos, BRAZIL
Iguaçu River
Santiago, CHILE
Montevideo, URUGUAY
Buenos Aires, ARGENTINA
Victoria, CHILE

*Walkabouts and wanderings took
Muir around the globe. A thousand-mile
trek to the Gulf of Mexico and journeys along the
Pacific Coast dominated his early life; in later years he
ventured to Europe, Asia, Australia, South America, and Africa.*

A R C T I C

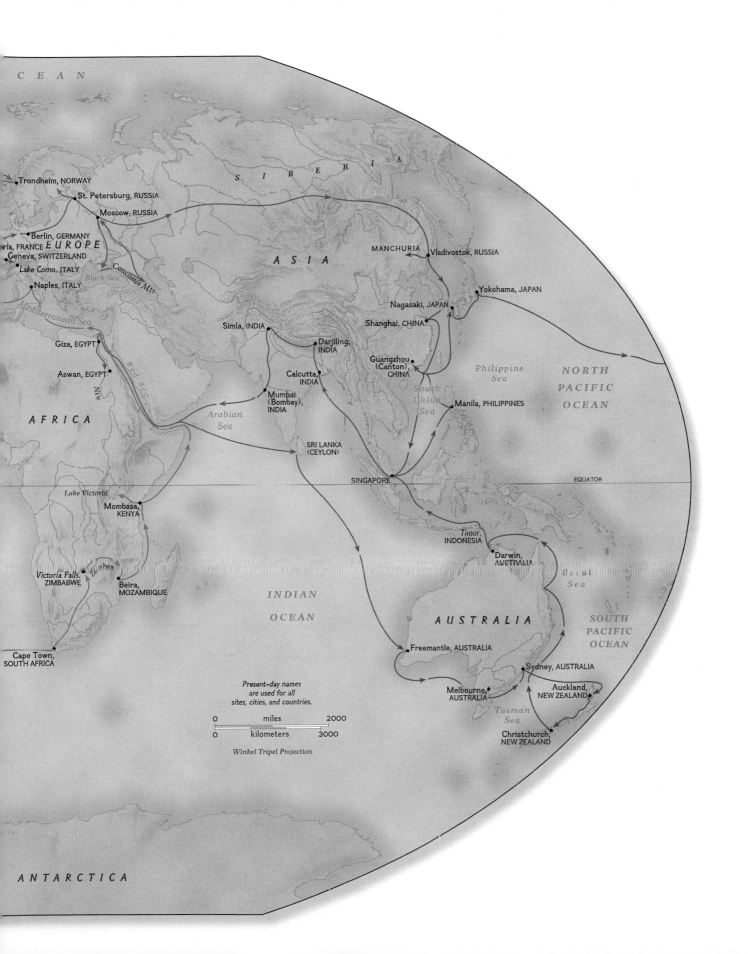

O C E A N

Trondheim, NORWAY

St. Petersburg, RUSSIA

Moscow, RUSSIA

Berlin, GERMANY

ris, FRANCE   *EUROPE*

Geneva, SWITZERLAND

Lake Como, ITALY

Naples, ITALY

Black Sea

Caucasus Mts.

S I B E R I A

A S I A

MANCHURIA   Vladivostok, RUSSIA

Yokohama, JAPAN

Nagasaki, JAPAN

Shanghai, CHINA

Simla, INDIA

Darjiling, INDIA

Guangzhou (Canton), CHINA

Philippine Sea

NORTH PACIFIC OCEAN

Mediterranean Sea

Giza, EGYPT

Aswan, EGYPT

Red Sea

Nile

A F R I C A

Arabian Sea

Calcutta, INDIA

Mumbai (Bombay), INDIA

South China Sea

Manila, PHILIPPINES

SRI LANKA (CEYLON)

SINGAPORE

EQUATOR

Lake Victoria

Mombasa, KENYA

Timor, INDONESIA

Darwin, AUSTRALIA

Victoria Falls, ZIMBABWE

Beira, MOZAMBIQUE

I N D I A N

O C E A N

Coral Sea

A U S T R A L I A

SOUTH PACIFIC OCEAN

Cape Town, SOUTH AFRICA

Freemantle, AUSTRALIA

Sydney, AUSTRALIA

Auckland, NEW ZEALAND

Melbourne, AUSTRALIA

Tasman Sea

0   miles   2000

0   kilometers   3000

Winkel Tripel Projection

Christchurch, NEW ZEALAND

A N T A R C T I C A

Settled by the Muir family in the 1850s, Hickory Hill in central Wisconsin remains the working farm of the Kearns family. John Muir helped his father build the barn (above) and other outbuildings. Like John, the Kearns's grandson helps with daily chores.

CHAPTER ONE

God and Hard Work

*John Muir
in his twenties*

"WHEN I WAS A BOY IN SCOTLAND I was fond of everything that was wild," John Muir wrote in *The Story of My Boyhood and Youth*. Thus began decades of outpourings—eight books, as well as journals, letters, and reams of unpublished manuscript pages—exultant, ardent, lyrical recollections of his ramblings in wild lands and his efforts to keep them wild.

John Muir's rapture began early in Dunbar, Scotland, a prosperous North Sea town of 5,000. A royal burgh at the mouth of the Firth of Forth, east of Edinburgh, the town was a place where John and his brothers and sisters could watch working schooners haul fish and goods up and down the blustery, storm-blasted coast; walk the narrow cobblestone streets; and bask in the shadow of the Lammermuir Hills. Young John's maternal grandfather, David Gilrye—a flesher, or meatseller—took him for short walks to look for spring flowers or to wander through a neighboring fruit orchard, where young Johnnie recalls savoring a fresh fig in the summer that he was three years old. In a haycock he uncovered a mouse with half a dozen tiny sucklings hanging from her belly. Another day, he reveled in the beauty of his Aunt Margaret's lily garden. "We imagined that each lily was worth an enormous sum of money and never dared to touch a single leaf or petal...." he wrote. In his provincial boy's world of farms and gardens, school yards and churches, an unquenchable appetite for life had begun to surface, despite a spartan existence. What was extraordinary was that a hunger for anything beyond a good meal and a warm room surfaced at all in a household where austerity was the norm and severity the disciplinary guide in child rearing.

IN SCOTLAND IN THE 1800s poverty and hunger were rampant, and children were used hard, whether in textile mills and coal mines or on farms, clearing fields, building rock walls, and helping to eke out a living in a relentlessly soggy climate. John's childhood was not spent amid the gentle English weather of Surrey or Sussex, with their soft breezes and drizzles, but on the northern half of an island battered by cold North Atlantic storms, with driving rains that could last for days.

Under dark skies and in dim rooms lit by candles and smoky peat fires, John's own father, Daniel, had found a bright release—in religion. He was in his teens when he was converted to a brand of evangelical Presbyterianism that allowed him to funnel all of his pent-up passions into studying the Bible. Salvation was what he yearned for, and any distraction from that effort was deemed frivolous and thus punishable. Yet, he did marry—twice. His first marriage was to a wealthy young woman who had inherited a feed and grain store in Dunbar. She purchased his release from the army so that he could run the business, and, when she died young, Daniel inherited the store. In 1833 he married young Ann Gilrye, whose father found Muir overly zealous and unbending. When the Muirs' children started coming—first Margaret, then Sarah, John, and David—Daniel continued the tradition of corporal punishment in which he had been raised. He considered it a cornerstone of their proper upbringing.

"A Scottish boyhood is a profusion of teaching and thrashing," John wrote. Yet nothing could dampen his boyish pranks, wild energy, and lust for the outdoors. When Daniel Muir told the boys, "Play as much as you want in the back yard and garden and mind what you'll get when you forget and disobey," his remonstrations went unheeded. John recalled: "Like devout martyrs of wildness, we stole away to the seashore or the green, sunny fields with almost religious regularity...."

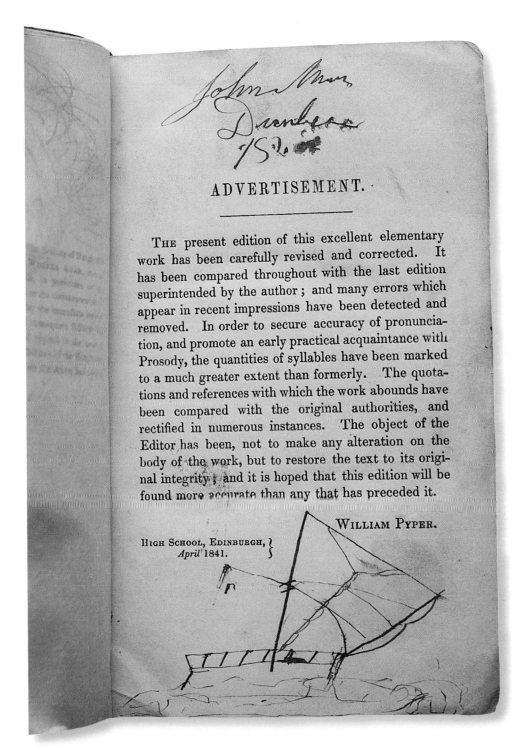

ADVERTISEMENT.

THE present edition of this excellent elementary work has been carefully revised and corrected. It has been compared throughout with the last edition superintended by the author; and many errors which appear in recent impressions have been detected and removed. In order to secure accuracy of pronunciation, and promote an early practical acquaintance with Prosody, the quantities of syllables have been marked to a much greater extent than formerly. The quotations and references with which the work abounds have been compared with the original authorities, and rectified in numerous instances. The object of the Editor has been, not to make any alteration on the body of the work, but to restore the text to its original integrity; and it is hoped that this edition will be found more accurate than any that has preceded it.

WILLIAM PYPER.

HIGH SCHOOL, EDINBURGH,
April 1841.

One of Muir's schoolbooks shows his early propensity to draw, a talent he would put to good use later in life. His Scottish school days were marked by the same discipline and severity that hung over his home life, but the joylessness seems to have had little effect on his high spirits.

JOHN MUIR: NATURE'S VISIONARY

The astronomer looks high, the geologist low. Who looks between on the surface of the earth? The farmer, I suppose, but too often he sees only grain....

~JM

Like strokes from an artist's brush, early morning mist tints the fields and forests of a modern-day farm not far from the Muir family's Wisconsin homestead.

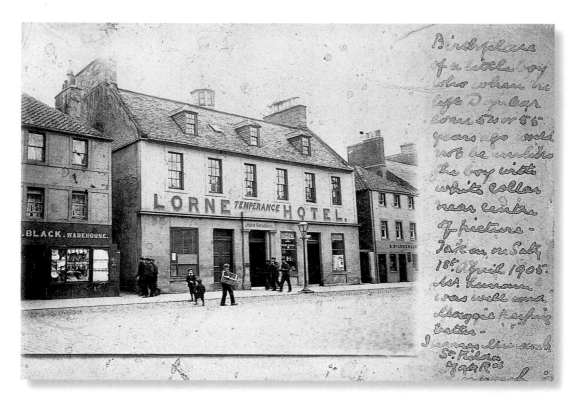

Before immigrating to America, the Muir family lived in Dunbar, Scotland, on the upper floors of a building later converted into the Lorne Temperance Hotel. "Like Scotch children in general," Muir later wrote, "we were taught grim self-denial." But Muir's childhood also had its bright spots, particularly while exploring the Dunbar coast (below) and taking walks through the countryside with his maternal grandfather, whose own love of nature had a lasting effect on the boy.

Prescient words for a boy who would later make his life's work walking beyond the boundaries of so-called civilization.

The daily beatings came like church bells, chiming out the hours and days of the young sinners' lives, but between thrashings young Johnnie, buoyed by an ardent curiosity and a robust love of life, eyed every facet and nuance of rock, river, flower, tree, cobblestone, and ship, and longed for more. Grandfather Gilrye taught his grandson what he could on their walks around town and down country lanes, pointing out the letters of the alphabet on shop signs and how to tell time on the clock at the town center.

In the spring, the huge garden out back took John's fancy. It was his parents' one mutual joy as well, and the children each were given a plot to grow whatever they chose. John spent hours contemplating the seeds, soaking them in water first so he could see the husks break and the sprouts begin, and later digging up a seedling or two to see how the roots formed.

The family enjoyed prosperity, and there were servants to help raise the children. Yet things were kept to a spartan minimum, more on principle than out of necessity. They lived on broth, boiled mutton, barley-meal scones, and potatoes; the portions, even of this meager fare, were small. Lighthearted by nature, Ann, John's mother, learned to suppress her spirits whenever Daniel was in the room. Whenever he was away, laughter and rambunctious play burst out, a reminder to John that you had to "catch fun on the fly," as a family friend later noted.

Dunbar was a castle town, and John and his brother David, two years his junior, loved to explore the thousand-year-old ruins. In winter, when darkness fell at four in the afternoon, they played a game under the bedcovers called "voyages around the world," in which they imagined they were traveling to such faraway places as India, America, Australia, and New Zealand—places that John Muir would in fact visit in his long life.

John began attending primary school when he was not yet three. He could already make out some words in his first book, and soon, under the tutelage and lashings of the schoolmaster, Mungo Siddons, he came to love the children's stories about wolves and dogs, priests and pirates. As if the lashings Mungo Siddons gave out weren't enough, the children turned the school yard into a battleground, where fights between "scholars," as students were called, were routine. They wrestled, bit, kicked, gouged, and punched each other when the schoolmaster was absent. The lads formed opposing armies and staged elaborate battles, as if the ancient heritage of the warring clans was still in their bones.

John Muir was a boy's boy, participating in fights and dares. "With stubborn enthusiasm we battered each other as if we had not been sufficiently battered by the teacher," he wrote. And the penalty for coming home from school with a black eye or torn clothing was yet another thrashing by his father.

At home, the games were just as strenuous. John and David dared each other to hang by their fingers from the second-story windowsill; they climbed trees, played with gunpowder, and fired at seagulls on the beach. In the spring they robbed songbirds' nests for their eggs. Once they captured a fledgling lark and caged it, dropping clumps of sod into the enclosure to re-create a meadow and catching plenty of insects for the bird to eat. But later, conscience-stricken, they released the young bird back into the wild. When there was nothing else to do, they ran races, "tests of endurance, running on and on along a public road…like hounds, without stopping or getting tired," Muir later recalled. They thought nothing of running ten or twelve miles after school, and, if they came home late, there was always another beating to end the day. But no punishment could keep them from their wanderings. "Wildness was ever sounding in our ears, and Nature saw to it that besides school lessons and church lessons some of her own lessons should be learned, perhaps with a view to the time when we should be called to wander in wildness to our heart's content," Muir wrote.

Grammar school was rigorous, with lessons in Latin and French, arithmetic, history, spelling, and geography. But it was the reading John loved most—a Scottish ornithologist's descriptions of fish hawks and bald eagles and John James Audubon's reports of passenger pigeons darkening the skies like storm clouds over vast tracts of the American wilderness, where pines towered and maple trees flowed with sugary sap. No place sounded as magical.

One evening the ever controlling Daniel told his children not to bother with their homework, because they would be leaving for America in the morning. The announcement of the imminent departure came to all as a complete surprise, but, while the boys reveled in the news, grandfather Gilrye was devastated by it. He would have to live out his remaining years alone, and he feared for what would become of the children: "Ah, poor laddies, poor laddies, you'll find something else ower the sea forbye gold and sugar, birds' nests and freedom fra lessons and schools. You'll find plenty hard, hard work." His words fell on deaf ears. Young John was too young to know that he was headed for years of hardship and servitude. To help stave off the inevitable, the grandfather handed each child a gold coin.

On the morning of February 19, 1849, Daniel and three of the older children— Sarah, John, and David—set out for the railway station in Dunbar and caught the train that would take them to the docks in Glasgow. It had been decided that Ann and their eldest daughter, Margaret, would stay behind with the younger children, Daniel, Mary, and Anna, until a house had been built for the family in America.

Daniel's mission was almost biblical. Like Abraham he "went forth....not knowing where he went." He had already run away from home once in his early 20s, escaping the life of hard agricultural labor he would have had to endure as a farmer. Now, he was headed into that life again. Unheedful of his father-in-law's warnings, Daniel could only feel the restlessness in his bones. He was materially comfortable in Dunbar, but other hungers in him had gone unallayed.

THE FAMILY SAILED ON AN OLD SCHOONER filled with eager immigrants on their way to various parts of America: the gold seekers to California; the Irish, Germans, Scandinavians, and Highlanders to New England or beyond to the Midwest—to Iowa, Illinois, Wisconsin, Michigan, and Minnesota. As evening fell, their ship glided down the Clyde River toward the open sea. Standing on deck, John Muir watched the lights of Scotland—of the Old World—fade. He would not see them again for almost 45 years.

The trip, which John dubbed "our wavering westward way," took six weeks. Leaving the seasick sufferers below, John and David spent the long hours of the Atlantic crossing on deck, talking to the sailors, learning knots and seafaring songs. They had spent their young lives watching with fascination as ships came and went from Dunbar. Now they were on one, headed for an uncertain destination. Daniel had originally planned to immigrate to Canada, but, after many vacillations and talks with other passengers, he decided to go to one of "the Western states"— Wisconsin, where the soil was richer and the climate far better. Also, the promise of a canal connecting the St. Lawrence Seaway with the Fox and Wisconsin Rivers could mean easy transport for his grain to faraway markets.

After landing in New York City, Daniel and the children traveled north up the Hudson River to Albany, then by Erie Canal packet through the Mohawk Valley west to Buffalo. From there, they caught a lake steamer to Milwaukee. Daniel hired a farmer with a draft team and a wagon to take them northwest to Kingston, in south-central Wisconsin—an area recommended by a family friend. It was spring and the frost was beginning to leave the ground. Their ponderous luggage from the old country, including farm implements, carpenter's tools, a set of scales, and huge wooden boxes secured with cooper's bands, frequently weighed the wagon down to its axles in the mud. They also carried with them a cast-iron cookstove they had bought in Buffalo.

This hill near the Muir farm became one of John's retreats, after the abundant "thrashings" meted out by his father, Daniel (opposite, top). A far more sympathetic parent, John's mother, Ann Gilrye Muir (opposite, bottom), sensed that her son would become an inveterate wanderer.

At Kingston the children were deposited in a rented room, while Daniel went out to locate a farmer he had been told of, who could help him find available farmland. Before the next day was over, the father had located an 80-acre tract with a lake on it near the Fox River. John Muir's wilderness life had begun.

"This sudden plash into pure wildness—baptism in Nature's warm heart—how utterly happy it made us! Nature streaming into us, wooingly teaching her wonderful glowing lessons, so unlike the dismal grammar ashes and cinders so long thrashed into us," John wrote. It was the beginning of April as the Muirs began their farming life, and the frozen world was coming alive again. Away from the gray gloom of Scotland, the sky seemed to tear open and reveal layers and layers of birds—blue jays, woodpeckers, hen hawks, kingbirds, whippoorwills. The lakes and river ice thawed and songbirds, Canada geese, ducks, and sandhill cranes arrived by the thousands. By day the birds were busy with nest building and in the evenings nighthawks filled the air with their eerie, whirring wing-sound. Snow clouds gave way to rain clouds. Wildflowers poked up through soggy ground.

The ground Daniel had chosen for a wilderness home was less productive than the grasslands farther east, but it was far richer in biological diversity because of its many lakes, marshes, and waterways. At the edge of Fountain Lake, John observed the shy snipe darting into the reeds to sing love songs and snakes writhing in the brush. Partridges drummed, bullfrogs croaked, and small green frogs "sang in concert, making a mass of music, such as it was, loud enough to be heard at a distance of more than half a mile." And in contrast to that loud marsh music there were "the many species of hyla, a sort of soothing immortal melody filling the air like light."

The wonder and solace Daniel Muir had found in the Bible and at church John found in the open sky and meadowlands lying between gleaming lakes like prayers. "The great thunderstorms in particular interested us, so unlike any seen in Scotland, exciting awful, wondering admiration. Gazing awe-stricken, we watched the upbuilding of the sublime...cumuli, glorious in beauty and majesty and looking so firm and lasting that birds, we thought, might build their nests amid their downy bosses...."

A summer thunderstorm mounting over a Wisconsin wheat field would have pleased Muir. "Storms are never counted among the resources of a country," he wrote later in life, "yet how far they go towards making brave people." Seemingly untouched since the 19th century, a straw hat rests on a bed of hay in a modern Wisconsin barn. Despite its utopian image, farmwork never appealed to John, who, from his teen years, constantly sought more from life than the plow and pitchfork.

While the children explored, Daniel and the nearest neighbors threw together a small shanty that served first as a human shelter until a house was built then as a barn for a team of workhorses used to clear eight acres of rocky land. They acquired a black-and-white dog named "Watch," a cat, and a pregnant sow. From a high bank of land the boys spied an Indian hunter, probably a Winnebago, on foot carrying a spear, which he thrust into muskrat dens (Muir called the animals "beaver rats"). The hunter ate the meat and sold the tiny skin for a dime.

When the children turned their eyes toward the earth from the bird-glutted skies, they saw snapping turtles and strange beetles and skunks, and small rodents of every kind. "Everything about us was so novel and wonderful that we could hardly believe our senses except when hungry or while father was thrashing us," John wrote.

Despite the reprieve from school, the severity of their father's discipline had not lessened, and Daniel's behavior seems heartless to contemporary eyes. "The old Scotch fashion of whipping for every act of disobedience or of simple, playful forgetfulness was still kept up in the wilderness, and of course many of those whippings fell upon me," John later wrote. "Most of them were outrageously severe, and utterly barren of fun." Besides the beatings, John was worked hard. Even when he had the mumps, his father sent him into the fields, where he "staggered with weakness and sometimes fell headlong among the sheaves." Yet John gives the distinct impression that the intimacy into which the Muir children fell with the land and animals and the joy that came from their ramblings and discoveries far outweighed any beating or cruelty their father could dole out. And it must be remembered that these were not acts of random violence but an acquiescence to convention, no matter how odious.

By the fall of 1849 the house was finished, and beef cattle, a yoke of oxen, and a team of horses—Nob and Nell—had been added to the farmstead, plus an Indian pony bought for $13 from the storekeeper in Kingston. John's mother, Ann, and the other brother and sisters arrived in the fall and soon the whole family—two adults and seven children—were once again under the same roof.

The boys' daily chores consisted of feeding the pets and livestock and fetching the cattle on horseback at sundown. For this job, they rode the pony, Jack, whose herding skills were so considerable that if the boys did not show up on time, he would go out on his own and bring the cattle back at a hard gallop. Ever the taskmaster, Daniel worked his animals as hard as he did his sons. At one point, he forced one of the draft team, the beloved Nob, to travel 24 miles on a sandy road in hot summer weather, driving her to exhaustion. When Nob came down with pneumonia and died from the misadventure, John was devastated. In his obituary for her,

The Bur-oak Shanty. Wisconsin Our first American home

An early sketch by John survives as the only image of the original Muir homestead. Erected in the summer of 1849, the primitive log cabin briefly served as the family home. Below, John's sister Sarah and her family pose in front of the Muirs' second Wisconsin home, a clapboard farmhouse at Fountain Lake.

Tilling his Wisconsin field with a draft team, a present-day Amish farmer mirrors John's hard boyhood. Muir deplored the havoc agriculture wreaked upon the wilderness. "The axe and plough were kept very busy…," he declared, "and in a very short time the new country began to look like an old one."

he wrote: "She was the most faithful, intelligent, playful, affectionate, human-like horse I ever knew…." The boy seems to imply that the horse's qualities exceeded those of some men.

On April 21, 1850, John Muir turned 12. Part boy and part man, he was by turns obedient and feral, plunging first into the intimacies of everyday life in the wilderness, then withdrawing far enough away to observe everything coolly. From a Canada goose, he learned an extraordinary lesson about loyalty. After shooting one in a flock, he marveled at the behavior of the flock's leader. "I shall never forget how bravely he left his place at the head of the flock and hurried back screaming and struck at me in trying to save his companion."

John had already learned hard lessons about self-denial, mortification of the flesh, forgiveness and punishment, and self-imposed exile, and he linked these grim realities to the "natural beauty-hunger" he felt—the healing, playful, solace-giving alms of the wild world, as well as the wise counsel and companionship of animals. He referred to his avian friends as "Wisconsin bird-people." "Too often the mean, blinding, loveless doctrine is taught that animals have neither mind or soul, have no rights that we are bound to respect, and were made only for man, to be petted, spoiled, slaughtered, or enslaved," he wrote. Thus began the rift with his father and religion that would ultimately send him walking.

As JOHN GREW OLDER, THE DAYS were more work filled. The family raised corn, potatoes, wheat, and a green fertilizing crop of English clover. All eight acres (more acreage was added later) were plowed with a horse-drawn rig, and weeds were hoed by hand. "No pains were taken to diminish or in any way soften the natural hardships of this pioneer farm life," John recalled. The house had no fireplaces, only the wood cookstove, and that was reserved for cooking meals, not to warm the rooms. Their boots froze during the night, and when they rose in the dark before dawn to begin chores, they had to stuff their aching feet into cold, hard leather. There was almost no meat at meals. Seeing them fairly starved, a neighbor suggested that meat would revive them, which it did.

The hardest work fell to John, since he was the oldest son and protective of his younger siblings as well. Not only was he the plowboy, but he also split rails for fences, chopped stumps out of the field, and oversaw everything his father did not have time to do himself. From dawn to dark they worked, getting up at 6 a.m. and

JOHN MUIR: NATURE'S VISIONARY

Of the many advantages of farm life for boys one of the greatest is the gaining a real knowledge of animals as fellow-mortals, learning to respect them and love them, and even to win some of their love.

~JM

A barn basks in the glow of spring sunset across the Wisconsin prairie.

Muir channeled his youthful energy into many ingenious gadgets and fancied himself an inventor before later turning to nature. His whimsical "hickory clock" (above), shaped like the scythe of Father Time, featured a pendulum with polished wooden arrows. Some scholars believe the Muir family homestead at Fountain Lake was the model for the bucolic scene on the face of his "sun clock" (far left). Among Muir's more whimsical inventions was a "loafer's chair" (left), which collapsed on the ground or triggered a pistol to shoot blanks if a slacker slumped in the seat.

going to bed at 9, all the while noting how such hard work was driving neighboring farmers to an early grave. John claimed that it stunted his own growth, even though he came to be nearly six feet tall.

When John was 19, his father bought another parcel of land about five miles southeast of Fountain Lake and began clearing it and building another house for the family. The new farm was called Hickory Hill. He sent young John out to dig a well by hand. When John hit rock his brother David began lowering him down into the hole in a bucket to chisel through the rock with hand tools. He would have to dig down 90 feet to strike water. But before he had finished the well, John almost died of asphyxiation from carbon dioxide that had collected at the bottom of the well hole overnight. Fading into near unconsciousness, he lay beside the bucket, listless. When his family called down to him, no answer came. Coming to his senses for a moment, John called for help and was hoisted out of the hole, gasping for breath. His first brush with death alarmed and awakened him. He was not someone to leave a project undone: Still woozy, he returned to work two days later. He proudly finished the well from which the drinking water for the house was drawn. But burning within him were new desires, not the teenager's lust for female companionship but a deep hunger for learning.

"I learned arithmetic in Scotland without understanding any of it, though I had the rules by heart. But when I was about fifteen or sixteen years of age, I began to grow hungry for real knowledge, and persuaded father, who was willing enough to have me study provided my farm work was kept up, to buy me a higher arithmetic," John wrote near the end of *The Story of My Boyhood and Youth*.

He was clever at everything he turned to and very quickly mastered the advanced math book. He then tackled algebra, geometry, and trigonometry. Along the way he discovered another passion: "I think it was in my fifteenth year that I began to relish good literature with enthusiasm, and smack my lips over favorite lines, but there was desperately little time for reading, even in the winter evenings…," he wrote. His father commanded that everyone be in bed directly after evening prayers, but John found a way to linger by the cookstove and read a few lines by candlelight. His father protested but finally said that John could get up earlier and read in the mornings. The boy took that permission to heart. From then on, he began rising at one in the morning.

"I sprang out of bed as if called by a trumpet blast, rushed downstairs, scarce feeling my chilblains, enormously eager to see how much time I had won…I had gained five hours, almost half a day! 'Five hours to myself!'…I can hardly think of any other event in my life, any discovery I ever made that gave birth to joy so transportingly glorious as the possession of these five frosty hours."

Until then, the household had owned only the Bible and a few religious books. Now John borrowed volumes, often from a kind neighbor, William Duncan. He devoured Shakespeare and the romantic poets—Cowper, Thomas Campbell, and Akenside—poets whose love of the natural world matched his own. He then turned his attention to Milton's *Paradise Lost*, whose verses he memorized and savored for the rest of his life. Reading in fits and starts, he branched out to Plutarch, George Wood's *Natural History*, then *The History of the Five Indian Nations*. He delighted in Mungo Park's *Travels in the Interior Districts of Africa* and Alexander von Humboldt's *Personal Narrative of Travels in the Equinoctial Regions*, in which the author sought to find the unifying principle that bound flora and fauna and geology together. After listening to John excitedly report on his readings, his mother said, "Weel, John, maybe you will travel like Park and Humboldt some day."

Like it or not, John Muir was undergoing an enormous and inevitable blossoming away from everything that Daniel Muir held true. He was flying fast toward the deep center of things, where his passion would take him into the heart of nature.

But not before he had dabbled in the world of machines and inventions. By the mid-1800s, the industrial age had come to the Midwest, and factories and foundries had begun to line the banks of its rivers. Agriculturalists had already gotten into trouble for leaping from subsistence farming to large-scale farming for profit. In ignorance, they quickly exhausted the fertility of their fields and cut down whole forests. They were duped by the promise of railroad and other transportation schemes that failed to materialize.

John himself caught the enthusiasm for the new and technological. His recently discovered love of books was joined by another passion—a love of inventing. The love was in part born of necessity. Too cold to sit for five hours in his frigid farmhouse with no fire, he went down to the cellar and began tinkering with bits of wood and hand tools.

Under the cover of night, in privacy and solitude, beneath the bedrooms of his sleeping family and with the "time wealth" his father had grudgingly granted him, John found he had a talent for things mechanical. He made a self-setting sawmill that could be placed in a stream to take logs as they came down the river. This was followed by waterwheels, door locks and latches, hygrometers, pyrometers, clocks, a barometer, an automatic hay feeder, lamp lighters, fire lighters, and a thermometer so sensitive that whenever someone approached it, it would register a change.

Perhaps it was the memory of Scotland and the daily walks past the town clock in Dunbar that inspired him to start making clocks: not just a face with two two dials, but a complex contraption all whittled out of wood and resembling an alarm clock. John called it "an early-rising machine." Then came a hickory clock "shaped like a scythe to symbolize the scythe of Father Time. The pendulum is a bunch of arrows symbolizing the flight of time. It hangs on a leafless mossy oak snag showing the effect of time, and on the snath is written, 'All flesh is grass.'" The next week he made Hickory Hill Farm its own four-dialed town clock, a device so big that it could be read by neighbors. After that, he came out with his most elegant invention, a star clock whose hand, a long spike with a star at the end, rose and fell with the rising and setting of the sun all year.

He had been in the fields for 11 years, and the wilderness he had so loved upon arrival in Wisconsin was now exhausting him. He had consistently risen to the challenge of physical hardship, and for the rest of his life adversity and learning were the fonts into which he dipped himself as he felt the longing for new challenges rise within him.

ONE DAY IN 1860, AT THE URGING of his supporter and neighbor William Duncan, John packed his wizardry into bags, slung them over his shoulder, and set off to enter the State Agricultural Fair in Madison, Wisconsin. He had never been away from the farm before, not even to Pardeeville, a tiny town only nine miles away. When the time came to say good-bye, he must have suffered a wrenching moment, much as he had when he had left Dunbar—and as his father must have felt on running away from home in his 20s. He was leaving a place he had come to know with an intimacy deeper than he would ever know again; yet that very place was suffocating him mentally. He had to leave. He had to gain the freedom to learn and explore, no matter how awkward and difficult—such was the magnitude of his gift. It literally carried him away.

On the eve of his departure from Hickory Hill Farm, John asked his father if he could count on any financial help from home. His father said no. It was now that the gold sovereign his grandfather had given him long ago was put to use. With that infinitesimal inheritance he set out on his own, never to feel that Hickory Hill was truly his home again.

JOHN MUIR: NATURE'S VISIONARY

As beautiful as an Arctic landscape, a Wisconsin winter wraps a rural farm. As a teenager, Muir loathed the harsh midwestern winters, but in later years, after several winters in the Sierra Nevada, he began to cherish the majesty and might of nature's frozen months. From mighty evergreens down to delicate prairie flowers (above), Muir was captivated by nearly everything he encountered in the woods and prairies that surrounded his first American home. "Wildness was ever sounding in our ears," he recollected of his Midwest boyhood.

At the state fair in Madison, his early-rising machine and thermometer proved immediate successes, drawing crowds to the Temple of Art, where the devices were displayed. At fair's end, Muir was awarded an honorarium, accompanied by high praise from the committee appointed to judge unusual exhibits: "The Committee regard him as a genius in the best sense, and think the state should feel a pride in encouraging him."

After the fair, Muir spent the late summer, fall, and early winter in the Wisconsin port city of Prairie du Chien. Then he returned to Madison and soon enrolled at the University of Wisconsin. He stayed for two and a half years, studying Latin and Greek, botany, chemistry, physics, geology, and mathematics. Summers he returned to work in the fields at Hickory Hill, cradling wheat and studying plants on the side. He earned enough money to see him through, though he subsisted on crackers, porridge, and water. He was befriended by Jeanne Smith Carr and her husband, Ezra Slocum Carr, a professor of chemistry and natural history. They would become lifelong mentors and friends.

By 1863, many young men Muir's age were being inducted into the Union Army to fight in the Civil War. John wanted nothing to do with the conflict, which he called "so unsightly a monster." He had planned to enter medical school at the University of Michigan in the fall, but in the meantime he decided to take off on a long botanical excursion. Walking down the Wisconsin River, he crossed the Mississippi, then roamed around the Iowa bluffs. That summer he returned to work on the family farm.

In 1864 a draft order signed by President Lincoln threatened to bring John into war, and so, at the urging of his mother, he took a train north, then walked through northern Michigan into Canada. Following in the footsteps of Henry Thoreau, John Muir became a draft evader, and what he would later call his "savage and all-engulfing appetite" began to emerge. ■

Sunrise erupts through a spring woodland in Wisconsin. "Everything new and pure in the very prime of the spring when Nature's pulses were beating highest…," Muir wrote.

Following in the footsteps of his famous kin, Muir's great-great-grandson Michael Hanna and his dogs head into the woods for a trek near his northern California home. Muir's own lifetime trekking began with a thousand-mile walk from Indiana to the Gulf of Mexico in 1867.

CHAPTER TWO

The Path Less Taken

John Muir
at twenty-five

IN 1863 AND 1864 THE CIVIL WAR WAS DEVOURING thousands of America's young men—the future nation builders, many of them immigrants like John Muir, who found himself exactly the right age for the draft. In the South particularly, many children were growing up with no men at all in their homes, except for the very old. The thought of war, any war, was abhorrent to John Muir, despite the fact that he had been a scrappy schoolboy fighter in Dunbar and a protective older brother at home. (He once bit a doctor who was giving his brother David a vaccination.) But what did the Civil War have to do with John? He was fighting now for an escape from a spiritual and intellectual confinement that, like the war, might just as easily kill him.

John had decided to enter medical school at the University of Michigan in the fall of 1863. He had escaped the draft once in 1862, when his name was not chosen. But the need for Union soldiers had increased, and President Lincoln had signed a new draft order, effective March 10, 1864. John decided it would be a good time to embark on another botanizing expedition. Taking a train on the first of March, he traveled from Wisconsin into Michigan, then he slipped quietly across the Canadian border on foot.

John had been an avid journal keeper since his early days at the University of Wisconsin, but now he went curiously silent. Little remains of that period in his life, except for some personal notes scribbled in a small, hand-sewn journal, recording the turmoil he was feeling at the time. All we know of his travels is that he wandered the edges of Lake Huron and Georgian Bay collecting plants, then worked for an immigrant family doing chores in exchange for room and board.

The war depressed him, and he was suffering physically from overwork and lack of proper nourishment. But the journals of Alexander von Humboldt describing his explorations in South America, one volume of which John carried with him, inspired John to dream of a botanizing journey to South America. Humboldt's words helped shape the young man's conviction that an overriding unity drew together the disparate elements of nature. While at the University of Wisconsin, Muir had been greatly influenced by the early conservationist, Increase A. Lapham. And from what he had seen in his local travels, he had come to understand that watershed forests and ground vegetation must be saved. Already the effects of the denuding in Maine and Michigan and the encroaching destruction of deciduous forests farther west could be seen—erosion and damage to the fisheries and fauna. Now the trees of Wisconsin and Minnesota were going.

With these ideas burning in his head, John began to wander, but he was not sure where he was going or why. His inventive genius was in conflict with his spiritual longings. He was pulled by passions he had just begun to define, yet he had to make his way in the world. How could he find a profession that did not harbor this conflict—the factory versus the wilderness, spirituality versus practicality? He wanted to make a contribution to society somehow, but it had to be on his own terms—that is, outside the conventions of a civilization that he felt showed no real concern for the happiness and well-being of living things and no regard for the world's beauty. There were days when he reeled with doubt: "I was tormented with soul hunger," he wrote in his small journal. "I began to doubt whether I was fully born....I was on the world. But was I in it?"

The lure of the farm and home was a steady hum in his ears, but the longing to leave what he called "the doleful chambers of civilization" banged even more loudly. It was always some wild thing that seemed to console him. One day in his ramblings, he came upon the wild bog orchid, *Calypso borealis*. "I never before saw a plant so full of life, so perfectly spiritual," he wrote, "it seemed pure enough for the throne of its Creator. I felt as if I were in the presence of superior beings who loved me and beckoned me to come. I sat down beside them and wept for joy."

This pencil sketch, one of the few relics of Muir's "lost years" in Canada, shows a maple sugar harvest. Muir went to Canada in 1864 to avoid military service in the Civil War and spent his north-of-the-border sojourn botanizing and toiling at an Ontario woodworking factory with his younger brother Dan.

John wandered all spring and summer in absolute obscurity, with almost no food. "By crooked, unanticipated paths, fast or slow, zigzagging like a butterfly," he made his way through Ontario to the Holland River swamps. He knew there was no straight course to salvation; he might as well have been taking advice from a Taoist sage when he wrote that his wanderings "whirl…like a leaf in every eddy, dance compliance to any wind."

While staying with a Scottish family in Canada, he learned that his Highland ancestors had been driven from the mountains of northern Scotland by landowners who wanted the area for sheep enclosures to supply their burgeoning wool industry.

JOHN MUIR: NATURE'S VISIONARY

Through every
vicissitude of heat and
cold, calm and storm…
we see that everything in
Nature called destruction
must be creation—
a change from beauty
to beauty.

~JM

*Lightning rends the sky over
Cumberland Island, Georgia,
as an Atlantic storm sweeps
across the palm-fringed coast
where Muir traveled in 1867.*

He could see plainly from the way the world was going that the disturbance of nature's economy encouraged wars, poverty, class struggles, droughts, floods, fires, and famine.

He knew he could not live without daily intimacy with untrammeled nature and mulled over ways he could live outdoors, "not as a mere sport or plaything excursion, but to find the Law that governs the relations subsisting between human beings and Nature." But first he needed a nest egg. His younger brother Dan, already in Canada avoiding the draft at his mother's urging, had joined John in September 1864; together they got jobs at William Trout's woodworking factory in Meaford, on Georgian Bay. Dan was immediately put to work at the sawmill, while John was given the job of inventing new machinery.

The Trouts, also of Highland descent, were ardent Christians and asked John to teach Sunday school. He said he would, if he could make the woods his chapel and laboratory. He found he had almost unknowingly dropped away from any kind of institutionalized religion. He wrote: "I never tried to abandon creeds or code of civilization; they went away of their own accord, melting and evaporating noiselessly without any effort and without leaving any consciousness of loss."

The need for enough money to feed himself required that he continue working. By the end of 1865 John Muir was inventing labor-saving machinery that could make broom, rake, and fork handles—2,500 a day, double the former output. By February 1866 he had made 30,000 of the things. But what was he doing with his life? At odds with his work for every obvious reason, his restlessness almost drove him to distraction. He was 27 years old, without a proper college degree, his plans for medical school evaporated, and he still did not know how to live in a way that would satisfy his passions.

On March 1, 1866, the Trout factory burned down, and the money owed to John for his inventions could not be paid. With a note from Trout for two hundred dollars in his pocket, he returned to the U.S., stopping in Indianapolis where he immediately took another job making carriage parts. As usual, he spent weekends in the woods, saving his money for his studies in the wild.

By the spring of 1867 John was still swinging like a pendulum between two worlds. He had reinstated his correspondence with Jeanne Carr, his friend from Madison, and he spent long days rambling in the wild. But he also loved the frenetic pace of inventing and putting his ideas into action on the factory floor. Even his machines created a philosophical dilemma for him. On the one hand, their purpose was to free humans from manual labor; on the other hand, as labor-saving devices, they often put people out of work. No matter what he did or where he went, he kept running headlong into the same kinds of paradoxes. But then fate intervened.

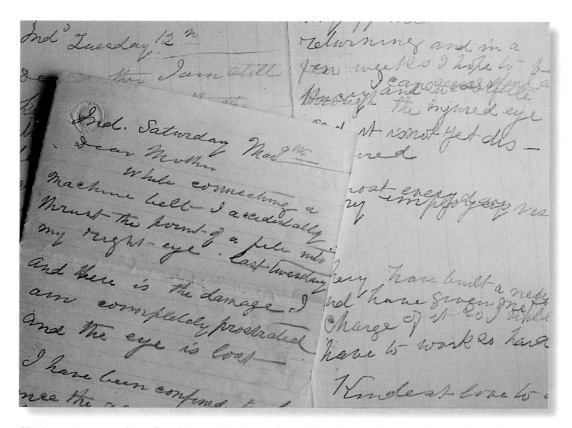

Muir's erratic penmanship reflects his anguished state of mind when he wrote this 1867 letter to his mother, explaining the accident that nearly left him blind. The mishap profoundly changed his life, prompting him to give up the factory life and pursue his love of wilderness.

One evening, while repairing a belt on one of the machines, John stopped to untie a connection with the point of a long file. Somehow, the file flipped up and struck him in the right eye. Stunned, he stood by a window holding his hand over his eye; the cornea was badly scratched and the aqueous humor dribbled out into his hand. His assistant, standing nearby, heard him say, "My right eye gone. Closed forever on all God's beauty!"

A specialist was called and assured John that, if he rested, his sight would be restored, at least partially. Muir was dutiful, staying in a darkened room for four weeks. Days no longer alternated with nights: Time floated and he drifted with it. In his dreams he imagined himself walking the Amazon Basin, as Humboldt had done. Then another image surfaced. He had seen an illustrated booklet about a place called Yosemite Valley in the Sierra Nevada mountains of California; he began dreaming of going there.

Finally, his eye was stable enough for him to go outside, and he headed for

JOHN MUIR: NATURE'S VISIONARY

I am well again, I came to life in the cool winds and crystal waters of the mountains....

~JM

Dawn creeps across the echoing Appalachian ridges of east Tennessee. Muir crossed these mountains early in his legendary trek to the Gulf.

the woods. For two hours he wandered, letting the world pour back into him—trees, weeds, rocks, birds, the light. He knew then that the machines he had invented stood between him and his true love, the wilderness. Soon he would see that the same genius and imagination behind those labor-saving devices could be turned to truly urgent matters: not industrial production but living the examined life, seeing into the nature of nature and capturing those sights in words.

When he returned to his Indianapolis lodgings that afternoon, he had come to a decision. "This affliction has driven me to the sweet fields," he said. "God has to nearly kill us sometimes, to teach us lessons." The stamina John had developed as a lad in Scotland and while working on the Wisconsin farm served him well now: He would walk and walk until he found his heart's home, and the rest be damned.

ON SEPTEMBER 1, 1867, WHEN HE WAS 29, Muir answered the call of the wild. He wrote to his friend Jeanne Carr: "I wish I knew where I was going. Doomed to be 'carried of the spirit into the wilderness'...I wish I could be more moderate in my desires, but I cannot, and so there is no rest."

As with every leave-taking, there were moments of sorrow, abject terror, and dread. He appeared at his brother David's store in Portage, Wisconsin, shoeless, wild-haired, dressed in ragged clothes. David, now a successful merchant and embarrassed by his brother's appearance, tried to find him a pair of shoes in the store, but none were big enough. Oblivious to his appearance, John was focused on the deep sadness he felt to be going, and he sensed he wouldn't be returning home again. As he was saying good-bye to his mother and sisters, his father interrupted to ask if John hadn't forgotten something. Then Daniel demanded that his son pay room and board for the weeks he had spent at Hickory Hill, helping with the harvest and saying farewell to his family. Dutifully but resentfully, John paid.

At the beginning of his journal, he wrote of his wanderlust: "In some persons the impulse, being slight, is easily obeyed or overcome. But in others it is constant and cumulative in action until its power is sufficient to overmaster all impediments, and to accomplish the full measure of its demands...." Later, on a more ebullient note, he continued: "All drawbacks overcome...joyful and free...I chose to become a tramp." The signature he wrote on the inside cover expressed his elation: "John Muir, Earth-planet, Universe."

Having shouldered the onslaught of loneliness that is the nemesis of every

A jubilant declaration of independence from the bonds that had shackled his childhood, Muir's signature on the inside cover of his journal for the thousand-mile walk carries a boundless home address: "Earth-planet, Universe." As to the alligators that crossed his path in Florida, he found them both frightening and fascinating, and in his journal (below) humorously wished that they be "blessed now and then with a mouthful of terror-stricken man by way of dainty."

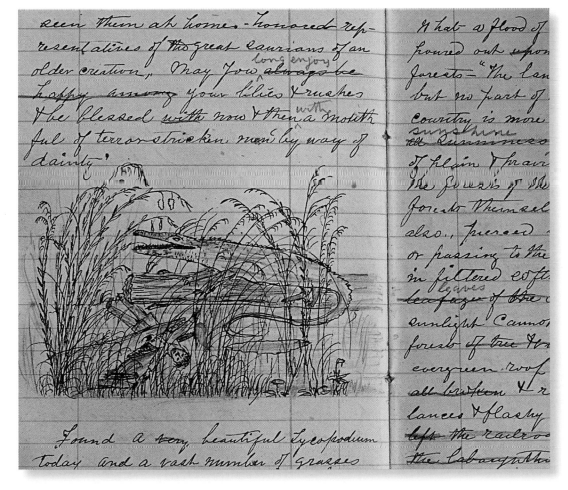

Muir intended to cross the vast Okefenokee Swamp (above) on foot, before he learned that the Georgia wetland was "a very sickly, entangled, overflowed, and unwalkable piece of forest." Altering his plans, he took a steamship from Savannah to Fernandina Beach in northeastern Florida. At right, live oaks shade a path in rural Georgia. By the time Muir reached that state's coastal plain, he was easily covering 25 miles a day, driven by the "tidal impulses" that perpetually spurred him on.

While waiting, John took a job in the sawmill, owned by a Mr. Hodgson, to earn a little travel money. On the second day there, he felt "a strange dullness and headache." The next day a fever broke over him "like a storm." He collapsed beside the trail he was walking but managed to struggle back to the mill. The night watchman thought he was drunk and left him alone. But the mill owner took him in. "I awoke at a strange hour on a strange day to hear Mr. Hodgson ask a watcher beside me whether I had yet spoken, and when he replied that I had not, he said: 'Well, you must keep on pouring in quinine.'"

John had walked and waded through the primeval swamplands of north central Florida, slept in the fetid heat, prey to every insect, and had contracted malaria. His long walk had come to an end.

CONVALESCENCE CAN SOMETIMES HOLD some of the sweetest moments in a busy life. When John was able to walk, he went straight to the edge of the woods and "sat day after day beneath a moss-draped live-oak, watching birds feeding on the shore when the tide was out." Birds had been a source of fascination all his life, and now, too weak to walk, he simply observed: herons, shorebirds, mockingbirds, crows, songbirds, gulls, pelicans, all of which he referred to as "feathered people."

During long, do-nothing days he reflected on the common origins of all beings and elements in the universe, "from the dust of earth," and wondered if plants and even minerals might not "be endowed with sensation of a kind that we in our blind exclusive perfection can have no manner of communication with...." In John Muir's world plants and rocks had souls, and humans were made of the stuff of lichens, mosses, trees, mountains, stars, and minerals.

When a working schooner, the *Island Belle,* stopped at Cedar Key for a load of lumber, John Muir made sure he was aboard when it left port, bound for Cuba. Still weak, he stood on deck through a blustery storm, letting cool water wash over his fever-wracked body. Once in Cuba, he found Havana labyrinthine and bustling, the air scented with flowers. January on the island was idyllic. Muir lived aboard the boat, and each day a sailor rowed him ashore, to the other side of the harbor where he could botanize. Back on the *Island Belle* for dinner he recorded his adventures "in the vine tangles, cactus thickets, sunflower swamps, and along the shore among the breakers."

A month later, still in poor health, he decided to push on to South America,

Nearly out of money by the time he reached Savannah, Muir slept in Bonaventure Cemetery for the better part of a week. As with nearly every experience he had along the way, Muir was bewitched. "You . . . are with Nature in the grand old forest graveyard, so beautiful that almost any sensible person would choose to dwell here with the dead rather than with the lazy, disorderly living."

Frozen in a flash of grace, a great blue heron takes flight along a Georgia shoreline. The biodiversity Muir discovered in the wetlands and woods of the American Southeast became rich fodder for his embryonic views on the relationship between man and nature. While tramping through the marshlands of north central Florida (right), Muir suffered from a "strange dullness and headache," an illness later diagnosed as malaria. Despite his poor health, he continued to explore, collecting plant specimens and jotting observations.

where he hoped to study the equatorial plants mentioned in the Amazonian journals of Humboldt. But no boat could be found and his dream of Amazonian adventures had to be put aside for a while. Instead, he took a "fruiter"—a fast schooner loaded with oranges—to snow-mantled New York. There, he spent about ten days, overwhelmed and largely unimpressed with the city. "I felt completely lost in the vast throngs of people, the noise of the streets, and the immense size of the buildings. Often I thought I would like to explore the city if, like a lot of wild hills and valleys, it was clear of inhabitants." Finally, he boarded another ship and traveled steerage class to Panama, crossed the isthmus by train, then boarded another ship and sailed for California. The plan was to stay in California only a short time before continuing on to South America. He should have known that fate would not stop meddling with him now.

Every mile that John traveled drove in the twin stakes of liberation and loneliness more deeply: Liberation from the bitterness he must have felt toward his father and loneliness as the miles and days severed the ties to the rest of his family more completely. But the thousand-mile walk to the Gulf had been the proving ground for what would become John Muir's life work: recording the natural history of California's Sierra Nevada and striving tirelessly to preserve it.

Some days on that walk he surely must have felt defeat. He was more vagrant than writer, and in lieu of his father's beatings, his own nature caned him into humility with footsore weariness, hunger, and malarial fevers. Inured to physical pain, Muir had made a "flower pilgrimage" that had caused his mind to blossom. He had read Emerson, and, like the great philosopher-poet, he too was becoming "a transparent eyeball." As he felt more sure of the path he had taken, he saw equality running through all things. And the more he saw, the more his appetite was whetted. The "martyred groom of wilderness" was walking deeper and deeper into the natural world. In so doing, he would discover himself in that world and the world in himself. Direct contact was what he longed for. Complete knowledge. "I am nothing...," Emerson had written. "I see all...." ▪

Simplicity of a Cuban church contrasts with the elaborate flora that Muir discovered on the Caribbean island. Unable to travel on to South America, his hoped-for destination, Muir settled instead on California—a decision that would change both the course of his life and the fate of America's wild lands.

Although sheepherding gave Muir an excuse to spend his first full summer in Yosemite, he came to deplore sheep because of the damage they did to the wilderness. "One would rather herd wolves than sheep," he wrote—a sentiment this present-day rancher probably would not share.

CHAPTER THREE

Range of Light

John Muir
in his mid-thirties

BY THE TIME THE SHIP CARRYING JOHN MUIR docked in San Francisco in 1868, he had befriended a British traveler named Chilwell, and together they walked into town. A now famous conversation ensued: "What's the quickest way out of the city?" John asked a carpenter on the street. "Where do you want to go?" the man asked. "Anywhere that is wild," Muir said.

They took the Oakland ferry across the bay and walked toward the Sierra. It was near the beginning of April when they followed the Diablo foothills south to Gilroy, then turned east over Pacheco Pass, crossing the broad plain running with horses and carpeted with wildflowers. As they walked, John exclaimed over every aspect of landscape along the way—the sweet stream music and lark song; the stacked, blued layers of hills and mountains as far as the eye could see; then the "vast, level, even flower-bed" of San Joaquin Valley. Muir had never been into high elevations and could not have imagined the alpine splendors he was about to see. Using the compass that had taken him through Louisville, across the Cumberland

Mountains, and through the swamps of Florida, he and Chilwell found Hill's Ferry and crossed the San Joaquin River. Then they began the long ascent toward Yosemite Valley, which he would later come to know as home. Pure in heart and often baffled by his own impulses, he let his feet be his compass and unquenchable longings his guide.

At Coulterville they bought tea and flour at Francisco Bruschi's general store and continued upward through Deer Flat and Crane Flat. Chilwell complained to "Scottie," as he called Muir, about the spartan diet, but Muir, who had grown up on such fare, ignored his friend and, being foot-hungry, kept walking.

Of his first glimpse of Yosemite Valley, we know nothing. For the first time in his life, the eloquent John Muir was speechless, leaving only a few notes and sketches of the time he and Chilwell spent there (the rhapsodic descriptions came a year later). Perhaps he was overwhelmed by its immensity and grandeur—the rock walls and waterfalls, the stands of giant sequoias. After eight or ten days they came down and took jobs in a farmer's fields in the valley, because they had both run out of money. John's malarial fever was replaced by another kind of delirium: a burning desire to return to the high country.

Still, he ran hot and cold on his new life in California. In a letter he wrote to his sister Annie, he complained of loneliness: "I cannot accustom myself to the coldness of strangers, nor to the shiftings & wanderings of this Arab life." He reprimanded himself for being childish, as if loneliness were a condition that would soon fade.

That summer Muir worked as a ranch hand and ferryman, and in the fall of 1868 he took a job on a ranch near La Grange. Chilwell had moved on, and John was on his own. His new employer, Pat Delaney, was an Irishman who had trained for the priesthood, quit to join the gold rush, then "retired" to ranching. In him, Muir found a friend with an educated mind. He treated John with respect and encouraged his roamings and observations. Muir had never considered the possibility of such freedom: He could work, jot notes, collect plants, make sketches, and still get paid.

At the beginning of winter "Smokey Jack"—John Connel—offered Muir a job herding sheep. So, at 30 years old Muir found himself living in a squalid cabin between French Bar and Snelling, among hills burned brown from heat; he was still unsure of where he would go next. He hated the sheep and pondered a trip to the Andes or a South Pacific Island. He had books sent to him by Jeanne Carr, and his list reflected a serious mind. Instead of Burns, Milton, and the Bible, he was now reading science: Lyell's *Principles of Geology,* Tyndall's *Hours of Exercise in the Alps,* Ruskin's *Of Mountain Beauty,* as well as works by Darwin, Emerson, Thoreau, and

In his obsessive quest to verify Yosemite Valley's glacial origins, Muir clambered up Matterhorn Peak and recorded the endeavor in one of his journals. An inveterate journal writer, Muir kept notes throughout his life on his daily observations and activities.

Walt Whitman. His reading deepened his understanding of how to interpret the landscape, how to forge insights from his heart's fresh inquiries, but his lessons came directly from the glaciers, rocks, storms, birds, trees, and streams of the mountains and the austerities they would impose upon him. Only they could teach him how to live, and, unlike other writers, who only dabbled in solitude and wilderness, Muir would eventually find a way to live in the solitude of the wild.

Heavy rains began in December and continued into February. The night a hundred sheep were lost, John, always aware of the way humans intrude upon and damage what is natural, wrote: "Man has injured every animal he has touched." In mid-February spring began to show itself in California's Central Valley, and sheep camp was moved to the foothills of the Sierra. The snow line rose like a white curtain below which a tinge of green came slowly into being; the granite took and held light and heat. "After our smoky sky has been washed in the rains of winter," he wrote, "the whole complex row of Sierras appears from the plain as a simple wall,

JOHN MUIR: NATURE'S VISIONARY

The last days of this glacial winter are not yet past....and the world, not yet half made, becomes more beautiful every day.

~JM

Dawn light fires El Capitan, looming above the snow-bound Merced River.

slightly beveled, and colored in horizontal bands laid one above another, as if entirely composed of partially straightened rainbows." The lure of the mountains had begun working on him.

He took inventory of the wildflowers that covered the valley floor with the lust that earlier California gold diggers had counted their earnings, calling the flora "solar gold." He calculated the density of flowers per square yard: 165,912 open flowers and a million mosses representing 16 distinct species; he reveled in the foothills made of stratified lava, describing the volcanic history as a book, each deposition a chapter made of days darkened by ash.

For almost 30 years Muir had been struggling to find what Emerson referred to as "an original relationship to the universe." A "calling" is rarely loud and obvious but more often a garbled whisper, inaudible and with no clear map. John had been following his feet, sometimes stumbling but now beginning to stride with an innocence, exhilaration, and tirelessness that would mark the way he saw the world. He was a walker and student first, a writer later, but already he was ordering his daily experience into "leaves of grass," pages of rock, chapters of a book of nature whose complexity was as deep and riveting as any novel's. Conscious or not, his vocation as witness, celebrant, and author had been decided.

WHEN JUNE CAME, MUIR FOLLOWED Pat Delaney's sheep up into the Sierra, the mountains he would come to call the "Range of Light." "We never know where we must go nor what guides we are to get,—men, storms, guardian angels, or sheep," he wrote in the exultant style of his journal, later published as *My First Summer in the Sierra*. On this trip into the mountains, Muir was accompanied by a shepherd and a St. Bernard dog. From the floral universe of the Central Valley, the "sheep-cloud," as Muir called the flock, walked through chaparral—a mixed, short forest of manzanita, buckbrush, and scrub oak—and finally into the high country of sugar pine, silver fir, and sequoia. Ignoring the disparaging remarks made by the shepherd, Billy, about everything they encountered, Muir kept craning his neck to glimpse the towering, snow-covered peaks.

All winter he had stood with his back to the Sierra peaks, much as he would to a peat fire, warming himself with their presence. In turn, they began smoldering in him. Now, with each step, he was leaving behind what he saw as the degradations of city life and the human bondage of ranches and farms. The foothills were his Jacob's ladder, though he did not know what led him. Poor, footsore, and bedraggled, he tied up his pants with a cord of braided grass and made meals of tea and hunks of the hard, unyeasted bread that he carried in his coat pockets.

As he gained altitude, the lack of oxygen, enervating to most people, worked on Muir in reverse: His energy increased, and the trees began to fashion themselves into some sort of gate through which he passed. Each step brought him closer to what he had imagined as both hearth and fire. In his journal he wrote, "We are now in the mountains and they are in us, kindling enthusiasm, making every nerve quiver, filling every pore and cell of us. Our flesh-and-bone tabernacle seems transparent as glass to the beauty about us, as if truly an inseparable part of it...." *My First Summer in the Sierra* was not about "going," as *A Thousand-Mile Walk to the Gulf* had been; it was about arriving.

"The air...is growing sweeter," Muir wrote as each step upward opened nostrils, ears, eyelids. In the meantime, Muir's employer, Pat Delaney, failed to bring any food. For the next two days the old hunger pangs gnawed at the two men, a reminder to Muir of how dependent "civilized" humans had become on "a wheat-field and gristmill," while Native Americans and subsistence hunters in the Arctic were able to survive on whatever they found. "Like caged parrots we want a cracker," Muir wrote, rankled by the chasm between the worldly and the spiritual, the tamed and the wild. How could a human uncover "original mind" and a life unencumbered by fabricated "necessities," he wondered.

Delaney did arrive with food, and, as soon as Muir's hunger was assuaged, the exaltations bubbled up. "Never while anything is left of me shall this first camp be forgotten. It has fairly grown into me, not merely as memory pictures, but as part and parcel of mind and body alike. The deep hopper-like hollow, with its majestic trees through which all the wonderful nights the stars poured their beauty. The flowery wildness of the high steep slope toward Brown's Flat, and its bloom-fragrance descending at the close of the still days...." All that, and he hadn't even been above tree line.

His mood was sometimes fiery, sometimes childlike, always astonished. He seemed to be lifted into the mountains, as if riding bursts of warm air, and every 500 feet gained brought deeper rapture. Because his father's abstemiousness had almost killed him, Muir was always redefining wealth: the "sun-gold noons" and "alabaster cloud-mountains" were "divine, enduring, unwastable wealth." They were all, it seems, that he needed to survive, except for his simple bread and tea.

On July 8, he heard voices: "Many still, small voices, as well as the noon thunder, are calling, 'Come higher.'" And he went, his vocation not precisely a calling from God, but from the divinity implicit everywhere in the wild. At 6,000 feet Muir and the sheep rushed through stands of manzanita whose smooth chocolate-colored trunks "seem naked." His ear was a tuning fork: River songs gave way to high-pitched stream arias, separate, then mingling as they fountained out of the highest peaks. Sometimes he pressed a hand down on a ewe's back, and it came up covered with lanolin, which he wiped on his dry face. He hated the way the sheep trampled precious wildflowers—columbine, larkspur, *castilleja*—but they were leading him and he was following.

O N JULY 9 HE WROTE: "Exhilarated with the mountain air, I feel like shouting this morning with excess of wild animal joy." The meadows were gardens and the trees through which they now passed—silver firs, yellow and sugar pines—arched over their heads like gothic spires; if he pressed his nose into the crenellations of bark, they smelled like vanilla. Sleep seemed wasteful when the night sky was lavish with stars, and the days filled the landscape with populations of small animals: Douglas squirrels barked at him as he passed under overhanging branches, and the birds were still "feathered people," as they had been to him as a child.

At 7,000 feet they reached the lower, tree-glutted end of Yosemite Valley, where the meadows were now "embosomed" by mountains, the nights were cold, and the stream that passed through sheep camp ran with "icy cold, delicious exhilarating champagne water." Outcrops of granite began to show, bare mounds like flesh that sparked in Muir what would become a lifelong curiosity about glaciers. How are mountains and valleys made, how are glacier erratics distributed, how does "mountain pavement" get so smooth?

Half a mile from camp he could finally look into Yosemite Valley. Rendered speechless on his first trip there, he now described the "walls of the temple" and "the psalms of the falls." The valley was "a grand page of mountain manuscript that I would gladly give my life to be able to read." Moral compunction within and wild lands without: Step by step Muir was mapping out "the etiquette of the wild," the ethic of how to live in the natural world. But there were difficulties. When Carlo the dog killed a woodchuck, Muir lectured the dog on not taking lives. Yet here he was, herding a band of ewes whose lambs would be killed for food. The irony did not escape him. He must find a way to return to these mountains on his own.

Following a Native American trail up the eastern rim of the basin, then turning south to the edge of Yosemite Valley, Muir, Carlo, Billy, and the sheep finally

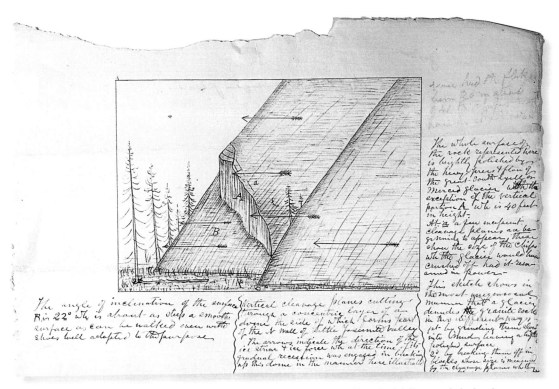

One of the first to speculate that glaciers were sculptors of the landscape, Muir faithfully recorded what he believed to be evidence of their chiseling might in his journals. Despite his convictions, Muir did not discover an actual glacier until he had spent a couple of years in the Sierra.

arrived. On a calm, sunny day John Muir stood at the brow of the massive cliff on the west side of Indian Canyon, and a rustic delight broke over him. "I shouted and gesticulated in a wild burst of ecstasy, much to the astonishment of St. Bernard Carlo, who came running up to me, manifesting in his intelligent eyes a puzzled concern…." Domes, spires, gables, battlements, precipices were "all a-tremble with the thunder tones of the falling water." With that roar in his ears he took off his shoes and socks and worked his way along the cliff toward the falls. Under the spell of the Yosemite "one's body seems to go where it likes," he wrote. Finding a narrow shelf from which to peer over the precipice, he grew dizzy and stuffed his mouth with bitter leaves to quell his giddiness, then crept down to the ledge. The view of the "snowy, chanting throng of comet-like streamers, into which the body of the fall soon separates" was sublime.

By mid-July they had established a camp on the valley floor; from here, Muir could watch morning and afternoon sun burn the rims of the domes. His bed was *magnifica* fir plumes, his sleep deathlike. Days were rambling bliss with no future, no past. Mammals, birds, and insects visited—deer, bears, grasshoppers, ants,

Snow-mantled boulders make white islets across the frigid Merced River as it flows through Yosemite Valley. With the onslaught of winter, most of Yosemite's human inhabitants headed for the low country. But Muir lingered, often alone, relishing the "starry crystals on every leaf and rock." Coyotes, too, winter over in the High Sierra, scouting snowbanks for hard-to-come-by meals. Despite their reputation as pests, the wily predators were among the animals Muir came to admire during his wanderings through the California high country.

Looking every bit the mountain man, Galen Clark poses at the base of the Grizzly Giant. Much like his friend Muir, Clark was a tireless advocate of protecting the area from commercial exploitation and twice served as guardian of the Yosemite Grant, as the preserve was called before achieving national park status.

mosquitoes, chipmunks, woodchucks, mountain quail, and blue grouse, all of which he studied, sketched, and loved. He observed the daily thunderstorms with interest. "The silvery zigzag lightning lances are longer than usual, and the thunder gloriously impressive, keen, crashing, intensely concentrated…." For a short time rain covered the ground with sheets of water, and, as he watched, he said, "How interesting to trace the history of a single raindrop!"

For the rest of the summer he drifted, sketched, took notes, and pushed himself beyond what he knew he could do physically, all with his employer's blessings. The days were "big…enough for a lifetime," he wrote. Weariness and time were banished, and he transcended every mountain obstacle—rock wall, rushing stream, and, later, even glacier and crevasse. As he climbed Mount Hoffmann and slept at Lake Tenaya, he came to feel "mountains are fountains—beginning places." He sensed a deepening union in all of nature, where everything "is hitched to everything else in the universe." With his notebook and a piece of bread tied to his belt, he went over the top and explored the other side of the Sierra, the eastern slope. His eyes roved over the desert floor and across the dead stubs of volcanoes around Mono Lake.

A month earlier he had written to his mother that "the deeper the solitude the less the sense of loneliness." For the time being he had relinquished all that was below—family, jobs, anything that did not pertain to the mountains. In the Sierra he had found a wide, wild home. "I have crossed the Range of Light, surely the brightest and best of all the Lord has built…."

By early September Muir, Billy, Carlo, and the sheep had begun their descent to the Central Valley, anxious to get out of the high country before the mountain snows began. "I must turn toward the lowlands, praying and hoping Heaven will shove me back again," Muir wrote, as he left the Sierra behind.

Muir spent the early part of the autumn working on Delaney's ranch, then he took a job as a sawyer and guide for James Hutchings, a hotelkeeper in Yosemite Valley. Muir's companion into the mountains this time was a young Philadelphian named Harry Randall, who had come out to work on Delaney's ranch. No longer footsore, Muir wrote to his brother before taking off again into the Sierra, "I start tomorrow for the mountains—the Yosemite…. I know that looking from the business standpoint you now occupy you will say that I am silly and imprudent, and that I value my time at too cheap a rate. Well, ahem, I have not time to make a long defense. The winter storms of the Sierra are not easily borne, but I am bewitched, enchanted, and must go…."

It was November 1869 and already wintry when they arrived. Hutchings hired young Harry to milk the cow, haul logs, and drive oxen; he put Muir on at the tiny one-man sawmill. The next day John and Harry built a cabin of sorts for themselves, situating it at the north end of the valley near the falls. Made of sugar pine shakes, it had a fireplace and floor of rock slabs, with ferns growing in the spaces between. Muir and Randall diverted a small channel from a brook to run through the cabin. The two young men slept in hammocks placed near the window, so that they could see the falls.

Muir's stay in Yosemite, which lasted until late 1872, was not a solitary retreat, nor was it meant to be. He was a tenderhearted and sometimes loquacious man, who valued human companionship. It was only frivolousness that he abhorred. Nearby stood the Hutchings's cabin, where James, his young wife Elvira, and their children lived, along with Elvira's mother, Mrs. Sproat, who knew Indian history and stories, made "memorable muffins," and helped out as the children were born.

Soon after Muir and his friend were hired, Hutchings left for Washington, D.C., on business and did not return for six months. In his absence, Muir and Elvira discovered that they had many interests in common, and they spent days together, comparing notes on plant specimens, taking hikes, reading the night sky. John found in Elvira Hutchings a kindred spirit. She was interested in botany and geology, as well as matters of the spirit. Her husband, who was much older, shared none of the same interests. Despite much speculation, no one knows the exact nature of the relationship between John Muir and Elvira Hutchings. She was married, and her mother was living in the house with her; her husband was John's employer, and Muir was careful not to mire himself in any human entanglement that might get in the way of his mountain ramblings.

From Elvira's mother, who had studied Indian nature signs and was recognized as a "weather prophetess," Muir began to learn some of the lore of the southern Miwok, a tribal group that had found its way to the valley centuries before. Yosemite had a rich Native American history. The first hunter-gatherers had come to the valley at least 6,000 years before. About 1,500 years ago, groups of northern and southern Miwok from the west side of the mountains began to come to the valley. Living in cone-shaped, brushwood shelters, they had a subsistence culture based on the acorn. Their villages spread along the Merced River on the valley floor, and the valley itself they called Ah-wah-nee, meaning "place of the gaping mouth." After a plague killed almost all of these people, the valley was uninhabited for some years. Then a mix of tribal groups led by Chief Tenaya reinhabited the valley. The white gold seekers and explorers called these natives the "Yosemites." The name came from a Miwok term meaning either "grizzly bear" or "some of them are killers."

In 1851, 17 years before Muir came to Yosemite, the Miwok had been rounded up and run out of the valley or killed outright by the Mariposa Battalion, an organized vigilante group funded by the government to remove Indian peoples to less desirable parts of the state. Muir made no reference to this horrific piece of American history—the removals and massacres that reduced the Native American population of California from 250,000 to 16,000. Nor did his wide sympathies specifically include aboriginal peoples. He had been disappointed by the demoralized Indians who passed through Wisconsin during his boyhood, seemingly ignorant of the holocaust they had suffered. Yet, having read snippets of Miwok and Maidu stories from Hutchings's guidebook, he made it a practice to greet Half Dome using its Miwok name, Tissiack. And he learned some of the other Native American place-names as well—Wakalla (Merced River); Pohono (Bridalveil Fall); Tutokanula (El Capitan); Kosuko (Cathedral Rock); and Cholok (Yosemite Falls).

MUIR HAD RETURNED TO YOSEMITE A DIFFERENT MAN. He was 31 years old, no longer a wanderer who had happened into paradise behind a band of sheep. He had set himself up as a student and recorder of natural history, though he did not yet know what he would do with his findings. Unlike the other men who had traipsed through the valley, Muir was not underwritten by any institutions. He wanted to live in the mountains full-time and preferred menial work in order to maintain his mountain freedom. On his days off he went to his real job: walking in the mountains.

While the prose in *My First Summer in the Sierrra* is lilting, by contrast the much later essays in *The Mountains of California* have a sense of gravity and seriousness of purpose, intermixed with the old intoxications of mountain joy. In the years spent in Yosemite, Muir would revolutionize the thinking about the effects of glaciers on mountain sculpting, reveal the life histories of water ouzels and sequoia trees, dissect geology in the Grand Canyon of the Tuolumne, study thunderstorms from the standpoint of a tree, contemplate the power of geologic forces during an earthquake, and, on the now famous climb of Mount Ritter, experience a mystic self-realization.

As the intoxication was trimmed back, he found that discipline helped his old struggle between the sacred and profane—the dualistic thinking of the 18th and 19th centuries—and led to a deeper revelation: That matter and spirit are not separate at all. He had read Emerson on the subject of unity: "Each creature is only a

Despite Muir's glowing descriptions, Yosemite's isolation limited tourism in the early days. Anyone hardy enough to make the two-day stagecoach trip from the railhead at Merced, by way of Wawona, was rewarded with the remarkable view from Inspiration Point (right). Above, a Muir sketch details the aftermath of a rock slide in one of Yosemite's side canyons. From a study of avalanches and earthquakes to thunderstorms and floods, Muir was an unremitting student of the forces that had conspired to create the valley.

Somehow most
of these travelers seem
to care but little for the
glorious objects about
them . . . . Blessed indeed
should be every pilgrim
in these holy mountains.

~JM

*Early tourists picnic among
giant sequoias. Innkeeper
James Hutchings, who
employed Muir as a sawyer,
brought the first party of
sightseers to Yosemite in
1855 and later operated the
Hutchings Hotel, the valley's
largest lodging.*

modification of the other; the likeness in them is more than the difference, and their radical law is one and the same. A rule of one art, or a law of one organization, holds true throughout nature. So intimate is this Unity, that, it is easily seen, it lies under the undermost garment of nature, and betrays its source in Universal Spirit." But unlike Emerson and other scientists and writers who visited Yosemite or wrote of the natural world with the same ideas in mind, Muir was not on assignment from a magazine or on a field trip funded by an academy or museum. He had made his home in a sugar pine shack, working as sawyer, carpenter, and part-time guide through all the seasons. Nor did he retreat to a city home when the snow flew; he neither had nor wanted one. As a result, "experts" who came to the valley routinely dismissed him as "a nobody," "a mere sheepherder."

Most of Muir's hours were spent outdoors. He hadn't begun writing his books yet, but he did keep copious notes in a trail-tattered blue journal and sometimes wrote with ink made from sequoia sap. Each year he became more gaunt, and his deep-set blue eyes took on a haunted look. The more he climbed, the shabbier his clothes became. His beard and hair were bushy and wild, and he declared, "I don't know anything of time and but little of space." He used his body to understand intellectual problems and his intellect to discipline his body to go farther on less fuel. He wasn't bothered with other people's opinions of him; his mind was "fertilized and stimulated and developed like a sun-fed plant." One by one he ousted the small daily obstructions in order to live unconditionally. "The remnants of compunction—the struggle concerning that serious business of settling down—gradually wasted and melted, and at length left me wholly free—born again!"

FROM MUIR'S EARLY YEARS at the University of Wisconsin, one person had mentored him: Jeanne Carr, the wife of Professor Ezra Carr. Now the Carrs were living nearby in Oakland, and Jeanne continued to send books and letters in which she encouraged Muir to publish his thoughts and findings. Later, she dispatched eminent visitors to meet him in his Yosemite home. While Muir may have been drifting from ridge to ridge, cloud to cloud, behind him lay a powerful woman who sent intellectual and emotional nourishment and guidance his way and planted the seed of his career as a writer. Muir received these guests in his "hang-nest" suspended over the river; it became a salon for the famous as Muir's own fame as an eccentric mountain genius began to grow.

In the early summer of 1870, Muir wrote to Jeanne Carr about his "Sabbath raids among the high places of this heaven"—walks taken in the high country on his only day off from the mill. "Would that you could share my mountain enjoyments! In all my wanderings though Nature's beauty, whether it be among the ferns at my cabin door or in the high meadows and peaks or amid the spray and music of waterfalls, you are the first to meet me and I often speak to you as verily present in the flesh."

Jeanne Carr kept promising to come to Yosemite—and kept failing to keep her promise. Instead, she sent great scientists and writers of the time to meet Muir. Joseph Le Conte, a geology professor at Berkeley, was one of them. In the summer of 1870, Muir spent ten days with Le Conte and his students, studying Sierra geology and enjoying the moonrise at Lake Tenaya, the high brown cone of Mount Dana, the flowers and cascades of Bloody Canyon. Muir and Le Conte became friends, and Muir took the professor on long rambles through Yosemite. So impressed was the academic with Muir's knowledge that he marveled over "a man of so much intelligence tending a sawmill!"

In May 1871 Jeanne Carr sent Muir her finest gift: Ralph Waldo Emerson. Accompanied by an entourage of family and friends from Boston, Emerson was traveling across the country in a private Pullman car. He was 68 by the time he reached California, and Muir was 33. As Emerson was being feted in the salons of San Francisco, Jeanne Carr wrote him about Muir and encouraged him to seek out this young genius of a mountain man.

"Emerson is here, Emerson is here," it was whispered around the valley the day he arrived. He and his fellow travelers settled in Leidig's Hotel, a two-story building that afforded a view of Yosemite Falls from its front porches. Muir later said that nothing had excited him more than seeing Emerson: "My heart throbbed as if an angel direct from heaven had alighted on the Sierran rocks. But so great was my awe and reverence, I did not dare to go to him or speak to him." Days went by while the Bostonians took in the sights on horseback. They rode up to Snow's Hotel, also called La Casa Nevada, situated so close to Nevada Fall that if the wind blew hard, the veranda became drenched in spray. When Muir heard that Emerson would soon be leaving, he finally acted. "In the course of sheer desperation I wrote him a note and carried it to his hotel telling him that El Capitan and Tissiack demanded him to stay longer."

Charmed by the fresh innocence of the plea, Emerson called for his horse the following morning and sought Muir out at Hutchings's sawmill. Muir recalled, "I stepped out and said, 'I am Mr. Muir.'" Muir had read Emerson's essay "Nature" two years earlier, and for Muir to share his afternoons with the famous transcendentalist was almost too good to be true. He invited the grand old philosopher up into his

The Mountains are calling me and I must go.

~JM

Living up to its romantic name, Bridalveil Fall spawns a plume of liquid silk. To the Miwok Indians, the 620-foot cascade was Pohono—Powerful Wind.

Muir's "jubilee of waters" floods a creek in Yosemite Valley. "How interesting to trace the history of a single raindrop," he once mused.

Trailblazing wilderness photographer Carleton Watkins, who took this photograph of Yosemite's imposing granite peaks, first ventured to Yosemite in 1861, seven years before Muir set foot in the valley.

hang-nest. "I had a study attached to the gable of the mill, overhanging the stream, into which I invited him, but it was not easy of access, being reached only by a series of sloping planks roughened by slats like a hen ladder, but he bravely climbed up and I showed him my collection of plants and sketches drawn from the surrounding mountains which seemed to interest him greatly…."

Emerson visited day after day, and, before leaving, invited Muir to ride out of the valley with his group as far as Mariposa Grove. Muir accepted the request with the promise that Emerson would camp with him in the sequoia grove. "At this he became enthusiastic like a boy, his sweet perennial smile became still deeper and sweeter, and he said, 'Yes, yes, we will camp out.'" Muir promised a huge campfire and a glorious night of star and tree gazing. But when they reached Clark's Station, the party stopped, and Muir was informed that it would be too dangerous for Emerson to sleep on the ground, as he might catch a cold. Muir protested, saying, "only in homes and hotels are colds caught, that nobody ever was known to take cold camping in these woods…." But his pleas went unheeded, and Emerson, like a good child, was taken indoors. "So the carpet dust and unknowable reeks were preferred," Muir commented.

Muir stayed the night with the Emerson party, and in the morning he took them up into the Mariposa Grove to see the giant sequoias. Mr. Emerson was alone occasionally, "sauntering about as if under a spell." Looking up into the trees, Emerson commented, "There were giants in those days." Some of the trees were so ancient they had been alive at the time when Jesus wandered the Middle East.

As the horses were being resaddled, Muir pleaded with the old philosopher once again to stay. "You are yourself a Sequoia. Stop and get acquainted with your big brethren." But the party got on their horses, Emerson with them, and rode away. Muir followed for a few miles, and Emerson stayed in the rear, the two men trying to stay in sight of each other. Muir said: "When he reached the top of the ridge, after all the rest of the party were over and out of sight, he turned his horse, took off his hat and waved me a last goodbye." Muir was alone again. "Gazing awhile on the spot where he vanished, I sauntered back into the heart of the grove, made a bed of sequoia plumes and ferns by the side of the stream, gathered a store of firewood, and then walked about until sundown."

Emerson was as shaken by the parting as Muir was. His other disciple, Thoreau, had died nine years earlier. Now, just as he had found another kindred spirit, he had to leave. A few days later, he appeared at the Carrs' back door on his way to the San Francisco ferry. He had become lost in the fog: "I could not go through Oakland without coming up here to thank you for that letter to John Muir," he said.

Muir was well-read in geology. He had the works of Tyndall and Le Conte and Louis Agassiz's *L'Etudes sur les Glaciers* under his belt. He had also read the Yosemite handbook written by the learned state geologist, Josiah Whitney, but with it he violently disagreed. After guiding Le Conte into the mountains for ten days to trace the movements of glaciers, he was quite sure that the branching valleys and canyons of the Sierra had been created by glacial scouring, but he needed more direct evidence. He needed to find a living piece of ice. And so he set out to find a Sierra glacier and solve the puzzle of how Yosemite was made. With allegiance to no one but himself, he pursued the truth with an ardor that was characteristically his own.

Everything in his life and thinking was pushing him farther into the Sierra. There was not a moment to be lost. He wanted to know, see, smell, touch everything, notice every change, walk under shadow, sun, storm. And he desperately wanted to understand how these mountains were made. Though the theory of plate tectonics was not part of geologic speculation at that time, some of the basic geology of the valley was already known or speculated: sediment deposition, the erosional force of water on steep mountain faces. On Muir's first summer in the mountains he had seen evidence of the ablation and accumulation of ice—glacial erratics, lateral moraines, the striations of glacial movement on granite. But it was not known then if a cataclysmic event or the push of glaciers had reshaped the Sierra.

In July Muir had quit his job at the sawmill. His friendship with Elvira had come to a grinding halt when Hutchings returned home. The two men had never gotten along, but now things were worse. Enthralled with his new freedom, Muir had exclaimed in his journal that he had "health so good I knew nothing about it, unmeasured time, and perfect independence...."

He spent the fall in the high country, where he undertook a thorough examination of all the basins and canyons whose waters passed through Yosemite Valley, in an effort to trace the pathways of every advancing and receding glacier. Hiking up massive canyons, over ridges to 13,000- and 14,000-foot peaks, he was doing nothing less than reading the history of ice, rock, and mountain building.

In September, Muir followed the northernmost tributary of Yosemite Creek to its source, where he camped in a grove of mountain hemlock near a lake, then explored the upper Merced basin. He walked along a ridgetop in a northeast direction "until suddenly halted by a sheer precipice over four thousand feet in depth." Standing on the brink of the south wall of the Great Tuolumne Canyon, he saw the crowded midsection of the Sierra peaks, how the opposite wall was really the shorn ends of ridges—the work of the Tuolumne Glacier—how the smoothed and sculpted precipices, the wide whale-backed ridges, and the spired peaks were all ground out and polished by moving ice.

IN HIS ROUGH TROUSERS AND HOBNAIL BOOTS, Muir covered hundreds of miles and thousands of vertical feet and in the process began taking on the appearance of a threadbare saint. His clothes were tattered, his face covered with campfire soot to dull the glare of sun and snow. Seemingly inexhaustible, he took in the elegant sweeping moraines that curved down from high amphitheaters of rock. He lay on polished Sierra pavement drinking tea from a tin cup and munching sun-hardened bread, his eyes filling with the skid marks and scourings of glaciers that had long ago retreated. When snow came, he fashioned a pair of snowshoes from tree bark and kept moving.

Some months before, Jeanne Carr had promised to come to Yosemite with her little boy. But a letter in August revealed that she had canceled her trip, and Muir wrote back: "I was so stunned and dazed by your last that I have not been able to write anything. I was sure that you were coming...I am lonely...."

Muir was suffering from the stultifying effects of solitude but could not see a way to change things: "Although there is no common human reason why I should

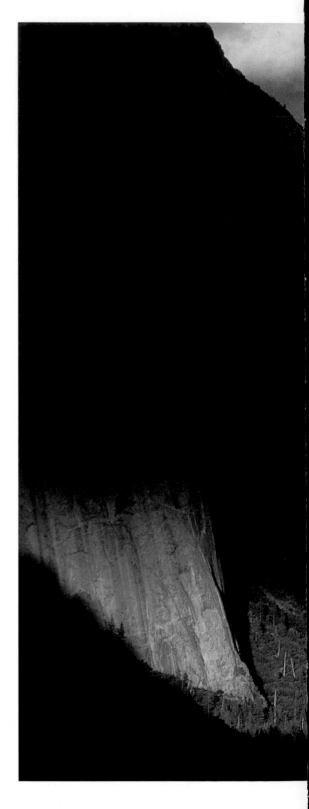

A masterpiece of light and shadow, Yosemite Valley glimmers beneath a cloud-filled summer sky. In an 1870 letter, Muir lamented the "tide of visitors" that flowed through the valley each summer; one can only imagine his reaction to the millions that visit Yosemite today. Muir attributed much of the valley's beauty to glaciation, and his sketch of Half Dome (above) shows how glacial forces shaped and sculpted the coarse granite into a polished monolith. "When Nature lifted the ice-sheet from the mountains," he declared, "she may well be said, not to have turned a new leaf, but to have made a new one from the old."

T hen it seemed to
me the Sierra should
be called, not the
Nevada, or Snowy
Range, but the Range
of Light.

~JM

*Like a sentinel guarding
the western flank of Tioga
Pass, 12,117-foot Mammoth
Peak is reflected in a Dana
Meadows pond. Muir herded
sheep in this area during his
first summer in the Sierra
but returned on solo treks
in subsequent summers.*

not see you and civilization in Oakland, I cannot escape from the powers of the mountains." In so saying, he counted on her understanding and continued love. "'No, dear friend,' you would say, 'Keep your mind untrammelled and pure. Go unfrictioned, unmeasured, and God give you the true meaning and interpretation of his mountains.'"

Muir was so completely absorbed with his studies of plants, trees, insects, birds, rocks, storms, and glaciers, he could not be derailed even by Mrs. Carr's urgent pleadings for him to come down to what Emerson, in a similar plea, had called "waiting society." They both admonished Muir not to hoard his findings; it was his duty to share them with the world. Muir knew this but he also knew that the mountain intimacy must go unbroken.

IN OCTOBER MUIR'S "ÉTUDES DES GLACIERS" came to fruition. He discovered a living glacier. He had been tracking the footprints of vanished glaciers like a hunter, following their marks up canyons to the uppermost peaks. One day as he walked the canyon between Red and Black Mountain, he reached the top of a moraine and came upon a living glacier: "The uppermost crevasse, or bergschrund, where the névé was attached to the mountain, was from 12 to 14 feet wide, and was bridged in a few places by the remains of snow avalanches. Creeping along the edge of the schrund, holding on with benumbed fingers, I discovered clear sections where the bedded structure was beautifully revealed."

Finally, he let himself down into "the womb" of the glacier, descending into "the weird under-world of the crevasse. Its chambered hollows were hung with a multitude of clustered icicles, amid which pale, subdued light pulsed and shimmered with indescribable loveliness. Water dripped and tinkled overhead, and from far below came strange, solemn murmuring from currents that were feeling their way through veins and fissures in the dark."

Head bowed, feet hobnailed, Muir had entered the life of all that is "other." He wrote such contemplations as "Thoughts upon Finding a Dead Yosemite Bear" and was constantly awestruck by the branching network of canyons and rock walls. He came to think of the mountains as works in progress, "becoming more beautiful every day." He contemplated what he called the doubleness of our lives: "Soul and body receive separate nourishment and separate exercise."

The journal notes he made while camping at "Lake Nevada, My Heaven"

Carleton Watkins's stunning images of the Mariposa Grove helped sway public opinion and government policy in favor of park status for Yosemite.

record: "Black mirror lake seeming to have a surface polish. Pulse of waters to show life. No wind, hush of rapids. Pure spirit white of curving shore...." Later that night he wrote, "A great dead log in the forest like a ghost—white on top, black with shadow beneath, that seems to lift it above the ground, and its whiteness glows almost like fire."

In exploring the glacier, the lateral moraines, the mica suns glinting in polished granite, the fractured summits, he was touching the origins of the mountains, and the melting ice was dripping and shining on his hands and forehead. His body was so attuned to mountain topography that he said he felt fit as a horse brought out to run, that his pack had become weightless, "unsubstantial as a squirrel's tail." Every inch of the mountains revealed past and present; they were an unwinding scroll: "Nothing goes unrecorded. Every word of leaf and snowflake and particle of dew, shimmering, fluttering, falling, as well as earthquake and avalanche, is written down in Nature's book.... The wing marks the sky." The Sierra was a place of meltwater and light, danger and initiation. In the process of learning about glaciers, he was, of course, delving into the nature of consciousness—his own and even that of the planet.

In what he called his "last raid of the season," Muir ran down into the Tuolumne Canyon and followed the river into Hetch Hetchy Valley. At the time, he could not know that valley would become a central battleground later in his life. For the time being, he declared it "one of Nature's rarest and most precious mountain temples." Yosemite and its environs weren't a single cathedral but a whole city of high altars.

When he finally returned to Yosemite Valley, a friend said that Muir looked like Jesus. St. Francis might have been more appropriate: He was surefooted, enraptured, and, having suffered cold and hunger, he had lost track of the notion of human comfort and gave himself completely to each day, to every mountain, as if carrying forward Thoreau's thinking, "One world at a time."

Perhaps it was frustration that made Mrs. Carr lash out at Muir for his obsession with glaciers. In December 1871, she referred to them as "pests" and to the ice ages as "horrible times." Muir took the jibes in good humor but felt the sting of betrayal. "Ice is only another form of terrestial love," he wrote, gently reminding her that the natural world cannot be separated into human notions of good and bad; if she cared for him, she must also love glaciers. He went on: "Glaciers *made* the mountains and ground corn for all the flowers, and the forests of silver fir, made smooth paths for human feet until the sacred Sierras have become the most approachable of mountains...."

Back and forth they went, until, finally, Muir put his voluminous notes together and wrote his first article. That winter he made his publishing debut. He was joining an august group of writers, among them Whitman, Thoreau, and Emerson, who had been pondering the same questions about nature and consciousness, spirituality and scientific discourse.

WHILE WHITMAN WAS SOUNDING WHAT HE CALLED his "barbaric yawp" from the East Coast, Muir began sounding his proclamations, not over Whitman's "roofs of the world" but over the peaks and glaciers of the world: "There is sublimity in the life of a glacier. Water rivers work openly, and so the rains and the gentle dews, and the great sea also grasping all the world. Even the universal ocean of breath, though invisible, yet speaks aloud in a thousand voices, and proclaims its modes of working and its power. But glaciers work apart from men, exerting their tremendous energies in silence and darkness, outspread, spirit-like, brooding above predestined rocks unknown to light, unborn...."

Muir's first article, "Yosemite Glaciers," appeared in the *New York Tribune* on December 5, 1871. As payment, he received the handsome sum of $200. The tone of his piece was gracious and spirited: "I have been drifting about among the rocks of this region for several years," he wrote, "anxious to spell out some of the mountain truths which are written here; and since the number, and magnitude, and significance of these ice-rivers began to appear, I have become anxious for more exact knowledge regarding them...," he began.

That winter Muir moved to Black's Hotel, a long low structure with a rose and honeysuckle-wreathed porch owned by an Englishman and his wife. There, Muir began writing in earnest, though not without grave reservations. In his new loneliness, he corresponded with Emerson. Emerson would list Muir among the greatest men he had ever met and wrote: "I have everywhere testified to my friends who should also be yours, my happiness in finding you—the right man in the right place—in your mountain tabernacle, and have expected when your guardian angel should pronounce that your probation and sequestration in the solitudes and snows had reached their term, and you were to bring your ripe fruits so rare and precious into waiting society." He invited Muir to roll up his herbarium, drawings, and poems and come to stay with him in his home in Concord, Massachusetts, where he would also be able to visit Asa Gray, a fellow botanist. One wonders how Muir could have refused such an invitation, but he did. Instead, he carried the first volume of Emerson's *Prose Works* with him in the mountains, and its heavily annotated pages tell the story of its value to Muir.

By February 1872, Muir had forgiven Mrs. Carr's displeasure with him and again made a fervent request for her presence in the valley. Anticipating the summer to come, he wrote: "I will mark off one or two or three months of bare, dutiless time for our blessed selves or the few good and loyal ones that you may choose. Therefore, at the expense even of breaking a dozen of civilization's laws and fences, I want you to *come*."

But she proved to be just as stubborn as he was. The more she urged Muir to come out of the mountains, the fiercer was his refusal. Finally, she promised that she would come to Yosemite that summer, and Muir's excitement grew once again. December had brought a winter storm, which Muir called "the jubilee of waters," but in March there was another kind of disturbance, "a glorious storm of the kind called an earthquake."

He sent a description of it to the Boston Society of Natural History: "For a minute or two the shocks became more and more violent—flashing horizontal thrusts mixed with a few twists and battering, explosive, upheaving jolts...." Part of the south wall shattered and an avalanche of boulders tumbled onto the valley floor "in a free curve luminous with friction...an arc of glowing passionate fire, fifteen hundred feet span, as true in form and as serene in beauty as a rainbow in the midst of the stupendous roaring rock-storm."

Everyone else in the valley fled; Muir stayed.

Instead of going down to Oakland, as Jeanne Carr had requested repeatedly, Muir wrote to her: "My horse and bread…are ready for upward," and off he went for two more seasons of tramping through meltwater and over roaring creeks during high water, carving passageways through wind-hardened snowdrifts; he even cut steps into the faces of living glaciers at 13,000 feet on both Mount McClure and Mount Lyell, so that he could plant stakes at the glaciers' edges and measure the yearly progress each of them made. Cold-season grasses and flowers stuck their heads out of fresh-fallen June snow as he went by, and there was the sound of water trickling everywhere.

During the summer of 1872 Muir continued studying and writing the history of ice, and as always he botanized, exclaiming over his beloved kalmia and primula. A steady stream of visitors came to visit him, including the geologist John Tyndall, the Harvard botanist Asa Gray, and a young family friend, Merrill Moores. Muir reveled in their company after long companionless winters but also found ways to strike out on his own. When he learned that the geologist Louis Agassiz, who was scheduled for a visit, couldn't come, he wrote: "I am learning to live close to the lives of my friends without ever seeing them." The periods of absence from visitors, when they occurred, proved to be a blessing. They gave Muir more time to explore the mountains at his own audacious pace, while the stream of letters preserved the threads tying him to the people he loved and respected.

IN OCTOBER MUIR WAS INDUCED BY HIS NEW FRIEND William Keith and two others to take a walk in the mountains for a last look at the alpine scenery before winter came. Keith—an artist and fellow Highlander whom Jeanne Carr had sent to meet Muir in Yosemite—had a specific landscape scene in mind to paint, and Muir knew where to take him to find it. They rode horseback up the Upper Tuolumne River toward the high massifs of the central Sierra, lake-studded, glacier-scarred, and crowded wildly together. The view suited Keith and they set up camp.

The next morning, Muir strode off, leaving the others behind. He was headed for the unclimbed "King of the mid-Sierras," Mount Ritter. "I could see only the one sublime mountain, the one glacier, the one lake; the whole veiled with one blue shadow…." To make his ascent, he was forced onto the glacier that swooped down from the top of Ritter.

Muir filled his journals with observations, sketches, and plant specimens collected in Yosemite. Like his other jottings, the text was often edited in later years to reflect changes in Muir's concepts and theories. Elvira Hutchings (left), wife of Yosemite tourism pioneer James Hutchings, shared Muir's enthusiasm for the wilderness, and their relationship long fueled speculation. Although the exact nature of their friendship remains cloudy to this day, the two were clearly close companions and confidants during Muir's Yosemite years.

"I moved on across the glacier as if driven by fate," Muir recalled. Then he climbed up an avalanche chute into "a wilderness of crumbling spires and battlements, built together in bewildering combinations, and glazed in many place with a thin coating of ice…." It was too dangerous to go back, so he kept climbing.

At about 12,800 feet he found himself at the foot of a sheer face in the avalanche channel. He considered his options, but there seemed to be none. He climbed straight up, grabbing handholds and footholds wherever he could find or reach them. Then he found himself at a point where he could not move at all. His arms and legs were outstretched with nowhere to go. He was sure that he would fall and anticipated "a moment of bewilderment…then…." He held on.

For a moment, he drifted, and his mind "seemed to fill with a stifling smoke." Suddenly, "life blazed forth again with preternatural clearness," he said, and he began moving effortlessly across the sheer face. "My limbs moved with a positiveness and precision with which I seemed to have nothing at all to do," he recalled. Clambering through rock above the chute, he found himself suddenly on the 13,157-foot summit.

From the top of Mount Ritter Muir could look out across the middle thickness of the Sierra, their braidwork and blue folds tumbling west into sun-cured bee pastures and east into desert mountains and dead volcanoes. Fear removed. The mountain perfect.

That year, Muir wrote in his journal: "The sun shines not on us but in us, as if truly part and parent of us. The rivers flow not past, but through us, thrilling, tingling, vibrating every fiber and cell of the substance of our bodies, making them glide and sing…." ■

Twilight gilds Horsetail Fall's thousand-foot cascade from the crest of El Capitan. Muir spent hours observing Yosemite's myriad waterfalls, admiring them from every angle in every light.

Earth-Planet, Universe

Their shaggy, cinnamon-colored bark contrasting with the whiteness of the rest of the forest, a grove of giant sequoias—trees Muir fought long and hard to preserve— weathers a fierce Sierra Nevada snowstorm.

JOHN MUIR: NATURE'S VISIONARY

Full of the "bounce and dance and joyous hurrah" that Muir revered in wild water, the Merced River dashes past dogwood trees in the Yosemite Valley.

Preceding pages: As a storm flees the Oregon coast, sunshine washes Crescent Beach in Ecola State Park. Muir enjoyed scrambling over the coastal bluffs, "as richly exciting to lovers of wild beauty as heart could wish."

JOHN MUIR: NATURE'S VISIONARY

Frozen poetry of a Yosemite winter holds 3,500-foot El Capitan and the Merced River in its thrall. A shameless cold-weather addict, Muir reveled in the winters he spent in the Yosemite Valley.

Preceding pages: Elowah Falls plunges into the emerald wilderness of the Columbia River Gorge in northern Oregon. Muir spent long hours pondering waterfalls, admiring them in every light and season.

JOHN MUIR: NATURE'S VISIONARY

G laciers, back
in their cold solitudes,
work apart from men,
exerting their tremendous
energies in silence and
darkness…. then they
shrink and vanish like
summer clouds.

JM

*Eclipsed by a colossal
landscape, members of the
Harriman Alaska Expedition
gather at the foot of Muir
Glacier. The lengthy 1899
field trip, organized by
railroad tycoon Edward H.
Harriman, afforded Muir
one last chance to probe
the Alaska wilderness.*

*Following pages: Morning
breaks over Yaki Point in
the Grand Canyon.*

Muir so loved the outdoors that he refused to have curtains on the windows of his bedroom at the family home in Martinez. He retired each night to a view of the moon and stars and woke up each morning to the rising sun.

CHAPTER FOUR

Settling Down

John Muir
in middle age

VOLUBLE AND CHARMING WHEN PEOPLE WERE AROUND, Muir nonetheless reveled in his life in the high country, with its days and months of relative quiet and solitude. It afforded him one of the only luxuries worth having—a way to look inward and to give back what he had learned. In his journal he wrote: "When we dwell with mountains, see them face to face, every day, they seem as creatures with a sort of life—friends subject to moods, now talking, now taciturn, with whom we converse...." But loneliness plagued him: "There perhaps are souls that never weary, that go always unhalting and glad, tuneful and songful as mountain water. Not so, weary, hungry me. In all God's mountain mansions, I find no human sympathy, and I hunger."

Two months after his revelation while climbing Mount Ritter, Muir went down, all the way to Oakland, his high-peaked *axis mundi* still wheeling inside him. Instead of binding him more tightly to his mountain fastness, his awakened mind ousted him from what had been his sanctuary, his university, his hiding place.

The middle ground meant human entanglements, but from now on, Muir would begin coming and going from his mountain life, until in 1875 he finally came down for good.

Muir's initial venture into society occurred in November 1872 at the urging of William Keith and Jeanne Carr. He was handed from friend to friend like a rare plant or some otherworldly specimen—from the Carrs and the Keiths to the Le Contes, the Stoddards and the McChesneys to Ina Coolbrith and Benjamin Avery, who had replaced Bret Harte as editor of the *Overland Monthly*. Nicknamed the "Faun," Muir was shuttled back and forth on the ferry between Oakland and San Francisco, up and down steep hills by trolley, to lunches, teas, and dinners. He thrived on the conversation and the interest everyone took in his eccentric life and the lyrical voice in his writing. The depth of his insights escaped no one: He was their West Coast Bartram, Whitman, Emerson, and Thoreau, all in one.

But the impact of any city on someone long in the mountains is crushing, and Muir soon complained of "the dust and din and heavy sticky air of that low region" and the numbing effects of the city. His feet hurt, he said—feet that had found their way previously over three countries, ten states, hundreds of vertical miles of mountains. Finally, he fled after "two weary homesick municipal weeks." When the train from Oakland let him off at Turlock in the San Joaquin Valley, he saw the mountains and headed off at a dead run.

EACH MOUNTAIN LEAVE-TAKING CONSTITUTED A DEATH for Muir and each return gave life again. He wrote: "I sped afoot over the stubble fields and through miles of brown hemizonia and purple erigeron, to Hopeton, conscious of little more than that the town was behind and beneath me, and the mountains above and before me; on through the oaks and chaparral of the foothills to Coulterville; and then ascended the first great mountain step upon which grows the sugar pine. Here I slackened pace, for I drank the spicy, resiny wind, and beneath the arms of this noble tree I felt that I was safely home."

Late in December, thrilled to be on "the living electric granite" once again, Muir suffered a serious fall while climbing the rock walls of Mount Watkins: "After several somersaults, I became insensible from the shock, and when consciousness returned I found myself wedged among short, stiff bushes, trembling as if cold, not injured in the slightest." The scrub oaks saved him from plunging down a cliff.

The "dead pavements" of the Bay Area became an important part of Muir's life as the 1870s progressed, but he was never content in the city. "There is not a perfectly sane man in San Francisco," he once griped.

Stunned, then angry at himself, he blamed his recent foray into the city for his sudden awkwardness in the mountains. Like a sailor, he had lost his mountain legs. He talked to his feet: "'There, that is what you get by intercourse with stupid town stairs, and dead pavements.' I felt degraded and worthless."

Muir must have felt that forsaking the mountains constituted a betrayal. He had turned his back on rock, tree, flower, bird, water, and bear people—his mountain friends. In self-punishment, he slept that night on bare rock with no pine boughs for his concussed head. "I slept on a naked boulder, and when I awoke all my nervous trembling was gone."

"Earth hath no sorrows that earth cannot heal, or heaven cannot heal, for the earth as seen in the clean wilds of the mountains is about as divine as anything the heart of man can conceive."

The fall from the mountain represented not a fall from grace but a crack in what had become a thick carapace. Muir exuded passion wherever he looked or stepped; he was susceptible and openhearted. He fell in love with every inch of the mountains, hanging about the skirts of Tissiack, gazing at changing cloud shapes,

fingering glacial polish, getting on hands and knees to inspect a flower, taking a whole day to watch an ouzel dart in and out of a waterfall. The place held him hostage: Every vantage point in the Sierra he took as his bride.

The fall on Mount Watkins served as a reminder, as all accidents do, that life is short, that we are fallible, vulnerable, mortal; that the panoramic view must always be kept in mind. Muir's calling was not simply to ramble free in the mountains but, after retreating from society, to come back as a celebrant and teacher. Unwilling and fearful, that is what he did.

By April Muir had 15 magazine articles completed or in preparation—but not without complaint: "I find this literary business very irksome," he confessed to his journal. Writing inevitably gave way to walking. In September Muir embarked on what would be his last major mountain ramble: along the entire length of the Sierra.

"The Mountains are calling me and I must go," Muir announced to Mrs. Carr. As if this was news. Accompanying him on the expedition were the botanist Albert Kellogg, naturalist Galen Clark, and a young painter, Billy Simms. As they set out on foot and horseback, Muir made daily entries in his journal of their progress. His eye had grown wider, and now he noted down the depredations caused by humans in the mountains as well as all that he found sublime. Despite this seeming contradiction, the sense of unity became magnified. He had Emerson's essays with him: "Nature can only be conceived as existing to a universal and not to a particular end, to a universe of ends, and not to one,—a work of ecstasy...."

They followed the South Fork of the San Joaquin River and camped in its basin. His first journal entry expressed outrage at the overgrazing of the meadows at Clark's Station. "The grass is eaten close and trodden until it resembles a corral...." Farther along, however, the vegetation was luxuriant. As always, Muir faithfully noted down the flora: wild cherry, sugar pine, willow, wild rose with scarlet hips, goldenrod, mint, yarrow, aster, columbine, larkspur, spirea, gentian.

Leaving the others, Muir climbed Mount Millar alone. He described the view of the Sierra cordillera from the summit as "one broad field of peaks upon no one of which can the eye rest....gothic near the axis—a mass of ice-sculpture." Muir kept walking, formulating in his mind as he went a picture of the entire ecology of the mountain range; from his perspective on high, the range resembled a tree with branching tributaries, with the main trunk as central axis.

They made camp in a small grass meadow on the edge of the North Fork Kings River, then wandered for a week in the sequoia forests. "The girth of 'General Grant' is one hundred and six feet near the ground...," he began then noted that it had been "barbarously destroyed by visitors hacking off chips and engraving their names...." Ascending from the first tributary of South Fork Kings River, Muir climbed two peaks in one afternoon and spent the night near tree line: "The moon is doing marvels in whitening the peaks with a pearly luster, as if each mountain contained a moon. I have leveled a little spot on the mountain-side where I may nap by my fireside. The altitude of my camp is eleven thousand five hundred feet and I am blanketless." When he returned to the agreed-upon meeting place, the others were gone, having left no food or horse for him. But he caught up with them. When asked why they left, they said they didn't think he was coming back at all.

October 15 found Muir attempting a first ascent of Mount Whitney. He tried first from the west side and once again found himself near the summit at night with no gear. "By midnight I was among the summit needles. There I had to dance all night to keep from freezing, and was feeble and starving the next morning." Three days later he tried from the east side and made it. He didn't leave his name in the tin can on the summit.

JEANNE CARR'S INFLUENCE ON MUIR was inestimable. Since his arrival in Yosemite five years earlier, she had undertaken the task of shaping his destiny. She had sent some of the best and brightest to meet him in the Sierra; she had urged him to condense his field notes into magazine articles, then encouraged him to send his work to editors; she sent him books to feed his mind then began haranguing him to come down from the mountains to join the world. Muir was beguiled by the force of her personality; who wouldn't be? Her final admonishment sounded puritanical: "You must be social, John, you must make friends…lest your highest pleasures, taken selfishly, become impure." At last, having been rebuffed so many times, she resorted to making Muir feel guilty for living a rich life that he loved, probably because it excluded her.

Finally, Muir gave in and made the move she had so long encouraged. Out of love for Carr? Loneliness? A deepened sense of mortality? Desire to evangelize, write, and publish? Probably all of those. By late November 1873, John Muir's Yosemite sojourn was coming to a close. How unsettling it must have been to pack up the herbarium, the collected rocks, notebooks, sketchbooks, and volumes of essays. He had once referred to humans as "rough vertical animals, sticks of filth," and now he was going to live among them. In a melancholy letter to his sister Sarah, he wrote: "I suppose I must go into society this winter. I would rather go back in some undiscoverable corner beneath the rafters of an old garret with my notes and books and listen to the winter rapping and blowing on the roof. May start for Oakland in a day or two."

Snow fell as Muir left his beloved valley, as if the sky itself were weeping for him. The plan was to stay with the Carrs—Jeanne was finally having her way. But ironically, a week before arriving, Muir found out that Jeanne and Ezra Carr's son had died, and, not wishing to be a burden, he found a room nearby at the home of other friends, the McChesneys. There, Muir spent the next ten months poring over journals, condensing those Sierra thoughts into publishable prose. In the evenings, he attended gatherings with an ardent circle of friends. Like it or not (and one suspects that after so much solitude, like-minded community was stimulating), a new life had begun.

HAVING ALREADY RANGED SO WIDELY—from Wisconsin to Canada, from Florida to Cuba to California and up and down the Sierra, Muir was no longer picking away at the details of mountain stratigraphy and glacial scourings but was widening his view to encompass the whole of America and its diverse citizenry. From natural facts, human meaning—that was the pathless middle way he was taking now, hacking truths out of the unending exultation he had experienced in his mountain home for so many years. In writing about a specific place he would teach readers to see the whole, healing, beautiful Earth. But the writing came hard.

While working on his glacier theories for "Studies in the Sierra," Muir voiced this opinion: "Everything is so inseparably united. As soon as one begins to describe a flower or a tree or a storm or an Indian or a chipmunk, up jumps the whole heavens and earth and God Himself in one inseparable glory!" he wrote. Then, "The dead bony words rattle in one's teeth." His new friend John Swett advised him to write just as he talked, which he did exceedingly well. Still, getting those "mist rags" into focus on the page remained difficult. But, as with everything, Muir pushed through the bad patches and his own obstinacy and wrote prolifically.

As if Jeanne Carr hadn't had enough influence on Muir, she now became his matchmaker. A Dr. John Strentzel and his wife, Polish immigrants, and their daughter, 27-year-old Louisa, visited the Carrs one day when John Muir was there. Jeanne had already written to Louie, as she was called, urging her to make Muir's acquaintance. Dark-haired and gray-eyed, quiet and retiring, she had forsaken a career as a concert pianist to stay at home. Dr. Strentzel was a well-known horticulturist with

Jeanne Carr, pictured here at a California cabin, was Muir's greatest benefactor, dispatching a steady stream of luminaries to his Yosemite retreat and bringing his writings to the attention of editors who would later publish them. She also played matchmaker, arranging the first meeting between Muir and Louie Strentzel, his future wife.

hundreds of acres of orchards and crops at his Martinez, California, ranch. Jeanne thought Louie Strentzel would be perfect for Muir. But the moment he sensed Jeanne's willful interference, he fled. Dreams of the mountains began filling his head, and, as soon as he finished "Sierra Studies," he packed his boots and heavy trousers and ran for the train station, shouting, "I'm wild once more!"

Yet when Muir arrived on the valley floor, he felt disconnected. "No one of the rocks seems to call me now, nor any of the distant mountains. Surely this Merced and Tuolumne chapter of my life is done.... I feel that I am a stranger here.... I will go out in a day or so."

He wandered about the valley, shaking the "dead pavements" from his legs and heart, then camped four nights at his "high altar"—Lake Nevada. Soon, the feeling of strangeness dissipated. Renewed and refreshed, having been welcomed at Black's Hotel by the old owl that had stayed close by during the earthquake the year before, Muir wrote to Jeanne Carr: "I have ouzel tales to tell....I am hopelessly and forever a mountaineer.... Civilization and fever and all the morbidness that has

Fascinated by every aspect of nature, Muir examines a conifer branch laden with cones during one of his voyages to Alaska. "When we try to pick out anything by itself," he mused, "we find it hitched to everything else in the universe." A favored haunt for thousands of sea creatures, the wave-lashed Farallon Islands (right) off the coast of San Francisco made the kind of wild Pacific scape that Muir loved.

been hooted at me have not dimmed my glacial eye, and I care to live only to entice people to look at Nature's loveliness. My own special self is nothing."

Muir stayed in Yosemite for more than a month. If the "Merced and Tuolumne chapter" of his life was over, he stanched the wound by ranging farther afield. In mid-October, on assignment from the *San Francisco Evening Bulletin*—the first of many such assignments—he made his way north on foot from Redding, walking the California-Oregon stagecoach road and heading for Mount Shasta. Alone and footsore, he spied the peak 50 miles distant and was instantly transformed: "All my blood turned to wine, and I have not been weary since." Despite his city living, John Muir had not changed.

I T WAS LATE IN THE YEAR FOR SUCH A CLIMB, and Muir could find no one to go with him. A local mountaineer, Jerome Fay, helped by packing in a week's worth of food and a few warm blankets. On November 1 the two men set out with several pack-horses. While they were still in the woods, the snow deepened and the footing was sometimes so bad that they had to unpack the horses, turn them loose, and camp for the night beside a bright fire, over which they roasted venison. Muir rolled himself in his blankets, slept for a few hours, then rose and set off for the summit alone: "The mountain rises ten thousand feet above the general level of the country, in blank exposure to the deep upper currents of the sky…," he wrote. The going was cumbersome, the bare slope was steep, and all along the way he was breathing "snow-dust" and often sinking to his armpits between loose lava blocks buried in snow. "I seemed to be walking and wallowing in a cloud," he wrote, "but, holding steadily onward, by half-past ten o'clock I had gained the highest summit."

On his way down a violent winter storm caught him. But no blizzard could close Muir's eyes or dampen his spirit. The stint in the city seems to have whetted his appetite for the extremes of mountain living. In the piled-up clouds he saw a "boundless wilderness," more land than ocean, as if the sky were another mountain range full of mysteries.

Exhilarated and undaunted, Muir made a storm nest at 9,000 feet, just at tree line. "I made haste to gather as much wood as possible, snugging it as a shelter around my bed. The storm side of my blankets was fastened down with stakes to reduce as much as possible the sifting-in of drift and the danger of being blown away. The precious bread-sack was placed safely as a pillow, and when at length the first flakes fell I was exultingly ready to welcome them." The storm lasted about a week. He reported that there were three inches of snow on his blankets and that he was visited by a friendly Clark's nutcracker. He was heartily disappointed when a fellow mountaineer, Sisson, who ran the pack station out of Shasta, sent Jerome Fay back up with a horse to "rescue" him.

But not for long. At the station, Muir met four hunters—one English, the others Scottish—who were looking for mountain guides for a wild sheep hunt. Muir, Sisson, and Jerome hired on, all of them carrying guns except Muir. It was December, and, while the others stalked wild sheep and antelope, Muir studied fossils and observed birds. Though he was a nonhunter himself, the generosity of his mind was such that he also understood the hunting spirit: "We little know how much wildness there is in us. Only a few generations separate us from our grandfathers that were savage as wolves. This is the secret of our love for the hunt. Savageness is natural, civilization is strained...." He published his account of this trip in the *Overland,* and it was later reprinted in *Steep Trails.*

On his way home Muir stopped to see an old girlfriend from college days, Emily Pelton, who had moved to Brownsville, in the Yuba-Feather River drainage of northern California. The morning after he arrived, a rainstorm broke, and the front carried gale-force winds. Ever spontaneous and deeply eccentric, Muir borrowed an overcoat, excused himself, went outside, and climbed a tree—his perch from which to enjoy the gale.

The published account of this experience in *The Mountains of California* helped bring Muir popularity, but the tree ride sounds hallucinatory: He "felt the light running in ripples and broad swelling undulations across the valleys from ridge to ridge, as the shining foliage was stirred by corresponding waves of air. Oftentimes these waves of reflected light would...seem to bend forward in concentric curves, and disappear on some hillside, like sea-waves on a shelving shore."

After the storm, Muir saw more clearly than ever that "we all travel the milky way together, trees and men." He was an immigrant and a walker after all and had already started his life over several times. Now, he was beginning again, and he grounded himself against the unknown deadness of a new "civilized" life by going out into wild storms. The more he was in the world, the more critical he became. He despised the idea that anything in nature is fearful or "soiled," or that nature is here only to be used by humans. He said, "How terribly downright must be the utterances of storms and earthquakes to those accustomed to the soft hypocrisies of society."

In February 1875 Muir returned to Oakland to write, working hard on a new batch of magazine articles. Despite his town living, he had managed to spend five months in the wilderness and in the next year would spend more.

By April he was back on Shasta again to make barometric observations for the Coast and Geodetic Survey. On April 30 he climbed the cone-shaped peak with young Jerome Fay. The storm that overtook them on the summit this time was life-threatening. The temperature dropped 22 degrees in a few minutes, and they were blasted first with thunder and lightning then with "crisp, sharp snow" that seemed "to crush and bruise and stupefy with its multitude of stings." They sought out nearby hot springs and lay in the steaming sludge to keep warm. Despite that, Muir, underdressed and ill-prepared, suffered frostbite. He cried the lament of many a mountain climber caught this way: "The ordinary sensations of cold give but a faint conception of that which comes on after hard climbing with want of food and sleep in such exposure as this. Life is then seen to be a fire, that now smoulders, now brightens, and may be easily quenched."

In May Muir returned to San Francisco to live with John Swett and his family. In June the two men, along with William Keith and J.B. McChesney, went to Yosemite. Still working as a correspondent for the *San Francisco Evening Bulletin*, Muir wrote with his usual fresh-eyed wonder about trees, giving them the dimensions of human character: Of the sugar pine, he wrote: "Many a volume might be filled with the history of its development from the brown whirling-winged seed-nut to its ripe and Godlike old age; the quantity and range of its individuality, its gestures in storms or while sleeping in summer light, the quality of its sugar and nut, and the glossy, fragrant wood...."

His notes jotted down on the trip were characteristically rhapsodic. He wrote of the sound of "ah-ing in the woods," the sound of an approaching storm; the "holy recesses in grove, mead, rock-mossy dells and cups made of...stones wedged together by some torrent"; the wild gardens of "Senecio and yarrow, dense mosses, Camassia, and Viola"; the "bird time of day" (morning); and the aged sequoias whose indestructible vitality can endure the hardships of weather for 3,000 years and more. "They are antediluvian monuments, through which we gaze in contemplation as through windows into the deeps of primeval time." But he also saw the infringements of human greed at "the temple"—land-grabbing schemes, the cutting of redwoods, overgrazing, he knew it all had to be stopped.

For the rest of the season, Muir went around and around Yosemite with various groups. With Keith, McChesney, and Swett he hiked the environs of Yosemite and over the top to the eerily arid Mono Lake and Owens Valley. In July it was to the southern Sierra and another climb of Mount Whitney; in August, he followed the Merced River. By September, the others had gone home and he was alone at last, except for his faithful mule, "Brownie." Together, they spent about two months in the southern Sierra, waking at "bird-time," listening to the owl, woodpecker, robin,

One of the most comprehensive portraits of 19th-century Alaska, Muir's journals are filled with descriptions of the territory's glaciers and other "noble, newborn scenery." He also sketched the Inuit (below), their oceangoing canoes and native dress.

A man who neither believed in God nor glaciers must be very bad, indeed the worst of all unbelievers.

~JM

Exploding with primal might, a calving glacier generates a pressure wave along the coast of Wrangell-St. Elias National Park.

bluejay, linnet, flycatcher, nuthatch, wren, plus buzzing bluebottles and "squirrel notes…mingled with the birds' earliest." Muir walked on grass, rock, and shadow, through groves of sequoia full of noon sunshine. "Compare walking on dead planks with walking on living rock where a distinct electric flash seems to attend each step," he wrote in his journal.

In Fresno Basin Muir came on a hermit living in a handsome cottage tucked away in a thick grove of sequoia. He'd been a gold miner, had lost his fortune, given up, and retired there. Muir found him sad, yet "finely alive to the silent influences of the forest pets, the mountain quail and the squirrels, talking to them as to friends, and stroking the tender sequoias a foot high, hoping they will yet become giants and rule the woods."

Muir had not been content to make a small arena of activity for himself: He was a tree-man, a sky-man, a bug-man, a rock-man; wandering the Sierra, "drifting through the gorges and woods" with wide-winged hawks heaving amid the towering cathedrals of sequoias, that had seen so many days, had imbibed so many centuries of sunshine. At night he contemplated the sculptural blackness of mountain walls with splinters of gleaming glaciers laid between. "The Milky Way is like a moraine of stars…," he noted in his journal.

Muir was a pilgrim and each step for him was holy and archival, each resting place giving sanctuary from the troubles and complications of the human realm. The writing in his journals near the end of 1875 took on the elegiac, bell-like quality of T'ang Dynasty poems. "Here is temple music," he exclaimed on October 20, "the very heart-gladness of the earth going on forever. On the Middle Fork of Tule I found a sequoia forest eight miles long, six wide, and wedge-shaped…. I saw flocks of ladybirds going into winter quarters."

Returning to his own winter quarters—the Swetts' house in San Francisco—he was surrounded by an instant family, with children, good meals, and conversation. But in the spring, summer, and fall, he escaped back to a wilderness he could call his own. Muir had dislodged himself so completely from his own family (he had not been to see his mother for 12 years) that it was no wonder he was lured into the homes and hearts of other people: Mother Carr, Daddy Swett, brother Keith. He'd drawn new bloodlines and felt happy in his adopted family's embrace. Gifts rarely come without a price. Jeanne Carr thought he needed more. Her persistence in matching Muir to Louie Wanda Strentzel was obvious to everyone. Why she wanted to give him a wife, no one can know.

Muir was oblivious, or pretended to be. He used his "just-down-from-the-mountains" innocence as a way of escaping such traps. He continued his studies. His examinations of the mountain world were still rhapsodic but had enlarged to include the wider realization that these wild places were in harm's way and must be saved. He wrote now for a public composed mostly of city people who would never live as he had lived. His voice took on a new tone, not one that had been politicized but one that incorporated his human community, a community that Muir believed could be taught to see and, through seeing, would learn to care.

"Everybody needs beauty as well as bread," he kept saying. He reluctantly accepted an invitation to speak to the Literary Institute in Sacramento in January 1876. His friend William Keith accompanied him and placed a painting on the stage. "Whenever you get frightened," he told Muir, "just look at this and you will remember why you are here." Muir did just that. Terrified at first, he then gazed at the Sierra landscape and was instantly transported. He spoke of the necessity of preserving the forest and the uses of beauty and against the presumption of human beings who thought that nature was made for their use only. More likely, he preached, it was the other way around.

AFTER THAT FIRST PUBLIC SPEAKING success, there were many other speeches and articles. Muir wrote a piece pleading with the government to help in a new conservation effort to save trees, warning that if nothing were done, all the trees would be gone.

His dispatches to the *San Francisco Evening Bulletin* continued that spring as he wandered through Utah. He stayed two weeks with Joseph Young, Brigham Young's son, and had an eye for one of his many daughters. The Mormons fascinated him, as they had Mark Twain and would later writers. Followers of the religion were living out a community experiment that combined theological elements within a regime of radical, self-governing socialism that delighted Muir. But in the midst of Mormon fecundity and family life, the old awkwardness returned: "Coming down from mountains to men, I always feel a man out of place; as from sunlight to mere gas and dust, and am always glad to touch the living rock again and dip my head in high mountain sky."

Muir's pace kept increasing, as if seeing more might make up for the loss of the year-round residency in his heart's home. He made excursions to the San Gabriel Mountains in southern California, where Jeanne Carr said she wanted to move (Pasadena was once a horticulturist's paradise of orchards, sun, and flowers), and another foray to Shasta, this time to botanize with the renowned Asa Gray. Leaving those high volcanic slopes behind, he took a skiff, drifting down the braidwork of

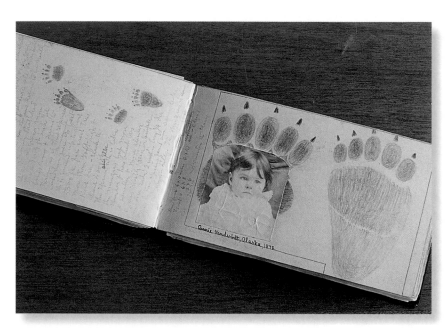

A blast of color in an otherwise monotone landscape, lupine and fireweed bloom around the edge of Vitus Lake, near the Bering Glacier in southern Alaska. "I never saw a richer bog and meadow growth anywhere," Muir wrote of Alaska's wetlands. Muir's journals are marvelous compilations of items he collected on his various trips. A page from his 1879 Alaska journal (above) blends his sketches of grizzly bear tracks and a photo of little Annie Vanderbilt, whose father co-managed the Northwest Trading Company in Sitka.

the Sacramento River. Later in the fall, he took a second river trip, this time along the Merced and San Joaquin Rivers. But amid all his travels, he made time to stop in Martinez and visit Louie Wanda Strentzel and her parents.

Muir's life had changed deeply in the last two years. He was still spending more than half the year in wild places but under totally different auspices. Now he was a journalist, lecturer, and guide, and part-time bon vivant. His monastic mountain fastness—his hang-nest—had been traded in for a room in a series of busy family homes; his life of contemplation and study given over to avid friend-ships and what in the 19th century must have seemed like frantic travel. Uprooted, enthusiastic, constantly adapting to new scenes, Muir was nonetheless torn between his old life and his new one. He announced to Jeanne Carr that he felt "some ten-dency towards another winter in some mountain den," but at the same time he was succumbing to her matchmaking scheme by beginning a long series of visits to the Strentzel household. And why wouldn't he? The ranch was capacious enough for all of them and was ideally perched between the city and the mountains.

Jeanne Carr was becoming increasingly remote in Muir's life: "It is long indeed since I had anything like a quiet talk with you. You have been going like an ava-lanche for many a year, and I sometimes fear you will not be able to settle into rest even in the orange groves," Muir wrote in a letter. Later he said, "I seem to give up hope of ever seeing you calm again."

As Muir shifted away from his old mentor, he turned toward the Strentzels. He may have dreamed of snowy winters in Yosemite, but he kept going back to the city. He needed an anchor, a family, a home.

He spent the winter of 1878 in San Francisco, giving lectures and writing— "Snow Banners," "Snow Storm on Mount Shasta," "The Humming Bird of the Cali-fornia Waterfalls," "Wind-storm in the Forests of the Yuba," "New Sequoia Forests of California," and "The Douglas Squirrel of California." Summer was spent with the Coast and Geodetic Survey in Nevada and Utah. He sent missives from Austin and Belmont and extolled the otherworldliness of the broad basins that lay between mountain ranges.

During the winter of 1879, Muir found a new room with Isaac Upham in San Francisco and worked on "The Bee-Pastures" for *Scribner's.* "When California was wild, it was one sweet bee-garden throughout its entire length, north and south, and all the way across from the snowy Sierra to the ocean," he wrote, as if speaking of his own wild life. He mourned the coming of plows and sheep to those "glorious pastures"—by which he meant the whole San Joaquin Valley—and understood, pre-sciently, that the destruction of those wild gardens would never find adequate com-pensation in the cultivated crops that had taken the bee-plants' place. He described

Until his harrowing adventure with a mutt named Stickeen, Muir had an ambivalent attitude toward domestic pets. But the Alaska escapade changed his mind. Here, he poses with a second Stickeen at his Martinez home.

the valley as "one smooth, continuous bed of honey-bloom, so marvelously rich that, in walking from one end of it to the other, a distance of more than 400 miles, your foot would press about a hundred flowers at every step."

In April Muir wrote Louie Strentzel a letter for the first time. Before he had finished, a box came from her: "Boo!!! aren't they lovely!!!" he wrote her enthusiastically. "The bushel of bloom, I mean…. An orchard in a bandbox…. A swarm of bees and fifty humming-birds would have made the thing complete."

In the meantime, he was busy lecturing to huge audiences about glaciers and took a crowd of 200 people to Glacier Point in Yosemite to show them how the valley was made. In June he was welcomed at the Strentzels like a war hero; he was becoming famous, and they knew how to flatter him. One evening, left alone by the Strentzels, John Muir proposed to Louie, and she accepted. In the morning, Mrs. Strentzel declared, "I don't believe there were ever four happier people in the world." A few days later, the now engaged Muir left for Alaska and didn't return until the following year.

Muir's unpublished diaries of 1879, titled "First Journey to Alaska," are reminiscent of his first summer in the Sierra. If that first summer was a baptism in the waters of wild living, then his trip to Alaska at age 41 offered salvation from what had become, almost unwittingly, a citybound, people-filled life. Muir would make seven long trips to the far north and spend a total of 22 months there. With the legendary dog Stickeen, he would come nose to nose with death, as he had on Mount Ritter. Alaska was "a new…world of ice with new-made mountains standing vast and solemn in the blue distance roundabout it."

IN JULY 1879, Muir slipped up the coast of British Columbia to the lush, forested, eagle-topped paradise of southeastern Alaska. Like a second marriage, Muir had taken Alaska as his own new bride. And it was in Alaska, after the social flurry and confusions of city life and the promise of marriage to a woman about whom he did not feel any driving passion, that Muir hit his stride again.

Nothing could ever blind him to the beauty of the world. If Muir had a badge of honor, that was it, and he wore it prominently: "So truly blind is lord man; so pathetically employed in his little jobs of town-building, church-building, bread-getting, the study of the spirits and heaven, etc., that he can see nothing of the heaven he is in." For Muir, no dust mote, no fungus or bug was too obscure to be beautiful, no rock too inanimate to show intelligence, no disaster too awful to reveal its inward divinity. Sailing up the coast on a mail steamer, he saw foggy clouds fondling and nursing leaves, beveled walls enclosing long rivers, islands broadcast like seed in oceans and bays, tree-gardens under pale, tender skies.

While cruising between Fort Wrangell and Cape Fanshawe, Muir claimed the whole coast as his "high altar." "Not a leaf stirring; deep, hushed repose; one bird, a thrush, singing sweetly, lancing the silence…. The whole blessed scene coming into one's heart as to a home prepared for it. We seem to have known it always." As usual, his time in the Alaska Panhandle was adventuresome. When they docked at

Fort Wrangell, the missionaries on board were greeted by S. Hall Young, a man of the cloth in his mid-20s. Young noticed the longhaired, shabbily dressed man on deck, absorbed by the view of the glorious encircling mountains, and sought him out. He was introduced to "Professor Muir, a naturalist." The two men shook hands, and from that moment a long friendship ensued.

Soon they were aboard the *Cassiar*, steaming north along the coast. Muir befriended the ship's engineer, Robert Moran, a roustabout Irishman whose ardent love for the wilderness was reinforced by his friendship with Muir. Moran himself would later be responsible for the preservation of a 10,000-acre tract of wilderness on Orcas Island in Puget Sound.

When they anchored at Glenora, a village on the Stikine River, Young and Muir sneaked off to climb Glenora Peak. Late in the afternoon Young fell and dislocated both shoulders. He hung precariously over an abyss, unable to save himself. Calmly, Muir reassured Young that he would be all right. Then Young heard Muir move away, whistling as he went. Soon, Muir was on a ledge below him and after some effort managed to pull him to safe ground. Muir set one shoulder, then supported and sometimes carried him back to the ship.

While Young recuperated, Muir plotted a canoe trip to Glacier Bay. In October, with a local chief named Toyatte at the helm, Muir was gliding north with one of George Vancouver's 1790s charts in hand. At the mouth of Glacier Bay, Muir recorded, "We made a cold camp on a desolate snow-covered beach in stormy sleet and darkness. At daybreak I looked eagerly in every direction to learn what kind of place we were in; but gloomy rain clouds covered the mountains, and I could see nothing that would give me a clue, while Vancouver's chart, hitherto a faithful guide, here failed us altogether." Indian villages and camps dotted the sandy shores. (Today, all one sees is grizzly bears). Inevitably, John made his way "upbay," where thundering outlet glaciers calved into quiet, iceberg-crammed waters. Towering above it all was Fairweather Peak (ironically named, as it is almost never visible because of bad weather). But it showed itself to Muir: "A red light burning with a strange unearthly splendor on the topmost peak of the Fairweather Mountains…. it spread and spread until the whole range down to the level of the glaciers was filled with the celestial fire….When the highest peak began to burn, it did not seem to be steeped in sunshine, however glorious, but rather as if it had been thrust into the body of the sun itself."

At the end of every fjord the icy faces of glaciers were breaking off in enormous splinters, thundering, sliding, splashing down into ink-dark water, then rising and floating slowly away. The bay was packed tight with icebergs that had to be pushed aside with an oar to make room for passage. Looking up from his low

How wonderful it seems that ice formed from pressed snow on the far-off mountains two or three hundred years ago should still be pure and lovely in color.

~JM

Ice teeters on the brink of a waterfall in the wild blue yonder of Alaska's Glacier Bay. Muir explored the area by canoe and foot in 1879.

vantage point, Muir reveled in this paradise of glacial activity, in the "wasting front," and the fossilized icebergs—unmelted shards, which he guessed to be a hundred years old or older.

One night, while everyone else was sleeping, Muir slipped out of camp and climbed the mountain that stood between two enormous glaciers: "The nearest glacier in particular was so distinct that it seemed to be glowing with light that came from within itself. Not even in dark nights have I ever found any difficulty in seeing large glaciers, but on this mountain-top, amid so much ice, in the heart of so clear and frosty a night, everything was more or less luminous, and I seemed to be poised in a vast hollow between two skies of almost equal brightness."

Eventually, Muir made his way home, but at a leisurely pace. He was a recalcitrant suitor at best, and, though Louie could not be thought of as the flame to which Muir was flying, she was bright and steadfast, and already trained in the art of waiting, which would be her lot throughout her life with Muir. Still, she probably wished it to be another way. In fact, she had posted several letters begging John to come home early—first for Thanksgiving, then for Christmas and the New Year. His reply ended simply: "Leave for the North in a few minutes. Indians waiting. Farewell." After that, only one more letter came; otherwise, the only communication from Muir to anyone was in the form of stories posted to the *San Francisco Evening Bulletin*.

Finally, at the end of January Muir wandered into San Francisco, not bothering to stop in Martinez on the way. It was February before he finally appeared at the Strentzels' door.

On April 14, 1880, John Muir and Louie Wanda Strentzel were married at the Strentzel house. John was almost 42 and Louie 33. If Muir had a faraway look in his eyes throughout the wedding festivities, it was because he was besotted with Alaska. After studying glacial history in the Sierra for years, Alaska's unexpected abundance of ice must have made his Sierra glaciers seem paltry.

For a wedding present the Strentzels gave the couple the original ranch house on the large property, and John moved his herbarium, rocks, notebooks, and books in. The day after the wedding John went into the fields to acquaint himself with the Strentzels' orchards and vineyards, setting to work immediately alongside the hired hands. Three and a half months later, at the end of July with Louie already pregnant, he left for Alaska again. Still, despite his skittish unconventionality and wanderlust, Muir would become a loyal and loving husband.

In Alaska, Muir took up his travels with his friend S. Hall Young, but he would make a new friend on the trip as well—a dog named Stickeen. (The dog bore the same name as a 335-mile-long Alaska river, a mountain range, and a native group.) Muir had never made much of domestic animals, because he felt that all the good

The only child of a Polish doctor who became a successful California farmer, Louie Strentzel, with her boundless patience, proved the perfect mate for Muir's restless soul.

sense and resourcefulness had been bred out of them. The little black dog with tan spots above his eyes, "an Indian cur," joined Muir, his companion Young, two Stikine Indians—Hunter Joe and Lot Tyeen—and a half-Indian named Smart Billy. Muir tried to send the dog back, but it refused to listen. They set off by canoe on a stormy summer day, and the dog "soon proved himself to be a queer character—odd, concealed, independent, keeping invincibly quiet, and doing many little puzzling things that piqued my curiosity. As we sailed week after week through the long intricate channels and inlets among the innumerable islands and mountains of the

God never made
an ugly landscape. All
that the sun shines on is
beautiful, so long as it
is wild.

~JM

*Seemingly aware of its own
majesty, a bald eagle surveys
the Alaska wilderness from
the crest of an iceberg adrift
in Glacier Bay.*

coast, he spent most of the dull days in sluggish ease, motionless, and apparently as unobserving as if in deep sleep. But I discovered that somehow he always knew what was going on. When the Indians were about to shoot at ducks or seals, or when anything along the shore was exciting our attention, he would rest his chin on the edge of the canoe and calmly look out like a dreamy-eyed tourist."

At the end of August Muir and his party set out to explore Taylor Bay. They left Taku Inlet, went north through Stephens Passage, crossed Lynn Canal, traveled through Icy Strait, followed Cross Sound, then finally entered the bay. There a three-pronged glacier terminated in an eight-mile-wide front; it was on this glacier that Muir and the dog would make their famous climb, later commemorated in Muir's book *Stickeen.*

It was August 29, late in the year, and a storm was on its way. "We set forth in the big gray day, letting the storm's hearty tides roll over us," Muir wrote with his usual confidence. "We were pulsed along in the very blood of Nature and could feel every heart-beat…. No silence anywhere, everything singing…."

The crevasse he came to was a "blue abyss," "a grave ready made." He had to climb down on hacked out steps, cross a silver sliver of ice, and climb back up the other side. The crevasse was too wide, or at least at the limit of what Muir felt he could jump. And Stickeen would have to jump it, too. "But poor Stickeen, the wee, hairy, sleekit beastie, think of him!" When the dog came to see what lay ahead, he gave John a strange look, to which Muir replied, "No right way is easy in this rough world." The dog sought another crossing but, finding none, came back.

With great trepidation, Muir climbed down one ice cliff, across a narrow sliver, and up the ice steps at the other end. Then he waited for Stickeen to do the same: "He hooked his feet into the steps of the ice-ladder, and bounded past me in a rush. Then such a revulsion from fear to joy! Such a gush of canine hallelujahs burst forth…. he rushed round and round in crazy whirls of joy…."

Muir returned to camp at 10 p.m., shaken and hypothermic. The others stripped off his wet clothes and fed him hot stew and coffee. He could barely eat and, though usually talkative, said nothing. Finally, he looked at the dog curled up on his bed. "Yon's a brave doggie," he said in his lilting Scottish accent. Hearing that, Stickeen opened his eyes and thumped his tail.

Muir and Stickeen said good-bye in Sitka. The dog was squeezed between Muir's legs. "You are a brave wee doggie," he kept telling Stickeen. When Muir stepped onto the pier, the small dog struggled. The Indians carried him back to the canoe, where he stood with his head leaning over the stern as he was being rowed away. Muir stood watching. Then he began his long voyage home to Louie.

After their day on the glacier Muir referred to Stickeen as his "horizontal brother." From the dog he learned that "human love and animal love, hope and fear are essentially the same." Muir had looked deep into the heart of that dog and saw that he and Stickeen were one and the same. "Those who dwell in the wilderness are sure to learn their kinship with animals and gain some sympathy with them, in spite of the blinding instructions suffered in civilization."

M
UIR'S LETTERS TO LOUIE DURING THE TRIP had been straightforward and emotionally telling: "I hope you do not feel that I am away at all. Any real separation is not possible. I have been alone, as far as the isolation that distance makes, so much of my lifetime that separation seems more natural than absolute contact, which seems too good and indulgent to be true."

In Martinez, Muir awaited the birth of his first child. At the end of March 1881, a daughter was born. Louie had been sick during the pregnancy, but the infant was healthy and there was great cheer in the Strentzel household. Muir loved dandling babies on his knee. (On his way to Glacier Bay, he had saved the life of a motherless baby by feeding him warmed cans of condensed milk.) Still, Muir did not fare well during his "ranch confinement." It wasn't fatherhood that began to kill him but being stationary. His wild heart was dying. He dropped to little more than a hundred pounds and suffered violent bouts of indigestion and bronchitis. He did not stay home long. By May he was on his way back to Alaska, this time aboard the U.S.S. *Thomas Corwin* to search for Captain De Long, a renowned Arctic explorer who had spent months on the northwest coast of Greenland. De Long was seeking a passage to the North Pole when his ship, the *Jeannette*, was lost at sea. *The Cruise of the Corwin* was taken from Muir's account of this five-month trip.

Once he had his sea legs, the fresh air gave Muir back what he called his "savage, all-engulfing appetite." He sketched madly and took notes as the *Corwin* came alongside the Aleutian Islands, huge black shapes buffeted by high winds and waves. From there the ship sailed north, passing through the Bering Strait into the Chukchi Sea, pushing slowly into pack ice.

Everywhere he looked there were new sights: sharp peaks fluted by avalanches, black-faced rock walls, jagged belts of ice in uplifted blocks lining the shore, groups of walruses massed on floating ice, snow drifting in sweeping curves over permanent pack ice, and behind, the white spires of mountains coming and going in a snow-bearing sky.

At Plover Bay, some Inuit hunters and their families boarded the *Corwin* to trade. One young mother proudly showed off her infant daughter, wrapped in skins, to Muir. The baby "looked gaily out at the strange colours about her from her bit of a fur bag, and when she fell asleep, her mother laid her upon three oars that were set side by side across the canoe. The snowflakes fell on her face, yet she slept soundly for hours while I watched her, and she never cried." What must Muir have felt, knowing he had left his own child at home?

On St. Lawrence Island Muir found that nearly two-thirds of the population of some 1,500 people had died of starvation during the winter of 1878-1879. "In seven of the villages not a single soul was left alive…," he recalled. "In the huts those who had been the last to perish were found in bed, lying evenly side by side, beneath their rotting deerskins. A grinning skull might be seen looking out here and there, and a pile of skeletons in a corner…."

On St. Michael Island, which the *Corwin* reached on the Fourth of July, a shaman was asked about the fate of the *Jeannette,* and he replied that "not only was the *Jeannette* forever lost in the ice of the Far North with all her crew, but also that the *Corwin* would never more be seen after leaving St. Michael this time, information which caused our interpreter to leave us, nor have we as yet been able to procure another in his place." The *Corwin*'s crew was undaunted and piled the decks with supplies, enough for nine more months at sea.

On August 16 in Point Barrow, Muir held a long-delayed letter from Louie in his hands and wrote back: "My Beloved Wife, Heaven only knows my joy this night in hearing that you were well. Old as the letter is and great as the numbers of days and nights that have passed since your love was written, it yet seems as if I had once more been upstairs and held you and Wanda in my arms…. I shall soon be home." And two months later, he was. It was the fall of 1881, and John Muir was 43. ■

Muir's Alaska adventures sparked a further bout of wanderlust that would take him through much of the Pacific Northwest. Awestruck by Washington's imposing Mount Rainier, he praised it as "the most majestic solitary mountain I had ever beheld."

At the Muir home in Martinez, California, Ross Hanna ascends the staircase leading to the glassed-in cupola where his famous grandfather once spent the early morning hours thinking and writing.

CHAPTER FIVE

John O' Mountains

*John Muir
in his later years*

JOHN MUIR CAME HOME FROM THE CRUISE of the *Corwin* in 1881 and stayed home almost continually for seven years. Down from the realm of the gods, he became an ordinary householder: devoted father to a growing family, loving husband, and excellent farmer. In all that time he made only two short trips to the mountains. Still long of beard and hair and dressed like a wanderer, he brooded silently as he toiled in the orchards, paid bills, supervised farmworkers, played with babies, fetched doctors, fixed carriage wheels, and picked, boxed, and shipped fruit. Like Ishi and the woman of San Nicolas Island—wild people who had been captured, brought into "civilization" and there died—Muir was in mortal danger as well. Increasingly jumpy, nerve shaken, and irritable, he developed a hacking cough and grew "thin as an old crow." Dutybound and inconsolable, he would not—he could not—set himself free.

Muir was no longer a wilderness man who lived the slow-pulsed continuum of seasons in the high country. He had gone headlong into society, and every year less time was spent in places where he felt free. To be married to such a man, Louie Muir soon realized she had to allow her husband his "mountain-time." Muir was used to making his way unencumbered; absolute togetherness felt indecent, as if human love was a rich dessert, succulent but unnecessary for the maintenance of life. Though his initial long absences in Alaska had felt like an abandonment to Louie, the steadfastness and loyalty he demonstrated throughout, home or away, gave her the strength to let him go. His well-being, both physical and mental, depended on it; he still preferred to have his home in a hollowed-out sequoia.

The marriage had a built-in flexibility not unknown in the last quarter of the 19th century, when men were setting out to explore unknown regions of the Earth: the Northwest Passage, the North Pole, Antarctica, Asia, Tierra del Fuego. Because transportation was by dogsled, skin boat, canoe, schooner, donkey, foot, and horse-drawn wagon, all journeys took months or years and those left behind exhibited a kind of patience rarely seen now.

L OUIE BUCKLED DOWN TO MOTHERHOOD and continued life on her father's farm in Martinez. She hadn't suffered a dislocation: Muir came to live with her and her parents. This meant that Louie had to mediate between John and his in-laws. The Strentzels did not understand that their son-in-law carried a whole mountain range in his heart (to which he had added all of Alaska). He simply could not live without the turning pages of the seasons, without the movements of glaciers, the comings and goings of birds. As farmers, the Strentzels were focused on their rows of cherries, apricots, pears, and zinfandel grapes; to them John's true lifework amounted to little more than idle wandering.

Dutifully, Muir dug in at the farm with his practical skills and his unflagging ardor. He turned the orchards around from an old man's horticultural paradise to a highly productive operation. Muir's fruit brought top prices. Muir drove his horse and buggy to the bank with sacks full of money stowed behind the seat. Everything Muir did, he did well. Soon, the Strentzel farms became profitable.

Ten years earlier, Muir's concerns about the health of the forests had been nagging at him. Although Yosemite had been made a state park by Lincoln in 1864, the boundaries were not being respected. Muir had seen enough devastation to know that more would come, and, finally, in 1876, he wrote "God's First Temples: How Shall We Preserve Our Forests?" for the Sacramento *Record-Union.* He had read

"Lock of Fathers hair Sent me by Joanna 1883," John's looping handwriting records of this wisp of curl. Scourge of the family, Daniel Muir ended his days separated from his wife and living with their youngest daughter Joanna in Missouri. Despite childhood memories of his harsh father, John was at the old man's bedside when he died in 1885.

Thoreau's *Maine Woods* and had embraced the idea of the sacred grove—remnant forests held back from the ax and saw. He had carried his volume of Thoreau to Alaska, but as yet, Muir had not grasped fully just what it would take to stanch the flow of trees from the mountainsides. Still, it was no surprise that in the winter of 1881 he was acknowledged in political circles as the spokesman for the Sierra and asked to help write two bills to be introduced in the U.S. Congress: One would enlarge the Yosemite Valley and Mariposa Big Tree Grove Grants, and the other would create a national park in the Sierra, most likely at the southern end, to help preserve the large groves of sequoias. Both bills failed.

In the meantime, work, children, and a litany of suffering among his own Muir relatives took most of Muir's time. By July 1884, Louie could see that John was clearly suffering from his recurring low-altitude illnesses—bad stomach and lungs. So Louie put their young daughter Wanda into the care of her mother and talked John into taking her to Yosemite. She had married a man whose heart's home she had never seen.

The trip was a not a success. Louie was afraid of heights, scared of bears, and

JOHN MUIR: NATURE'S VISIONARY

One learns that the world, though made, is yet being made. That this is still the morning of creation.

~JM

Churning a colossal path to the sea, the Columbia River provided Muir more proof of glacial sculpting. While geologists believed the river had cut its own bed, Muir was convinced glaciers had done it.

did not want to sleep on the ground. Both of the first-time parents were afraid to wander too far from the telegraph office, in case Wanda became ill. They soon went home. Later in the year, Muir's sister Annie visited; sisters Margaret and Sarah had come two winters before.

ANOTHER YEAR OF RANCH WORK AND VERY LITTLE WRITING went by. In August 1885 John suddenly felt he must see his father before the old man died. With little ado, he packed to go. By this time Louie was completely her husband's ally and urged him to stop in the mountains along the way. He did. Mount Shasta was his first stop. Then in Wyoming he spent a week with a newlywed couple on a pack trip through Yellowstone. He was sick along the way and bucked off by a dude horse, but his sense of humor, if nothing else, was returning.

Muir continued on to Wisconsin, to visit his mother and siblings. He had not seen any of them for nearly 18 years. One brother-in-law had died, a sister-in-law would soon be dead, and his mother was old and frail. His father, Daniel, long since separated from his wife for a life of evangelizing in Canada, now lived with the youngest daughter in Kansas City and was dying. As the family gathered around Daniel's bed, Muir found that his father had had a change of heart: He had apologized for the "cruel mistakes" he had made and for the brutal beatings he had dispensed; he counseled Joanna not to raise her own children that way.

Not long after John's arrival, the end came. He wrote of it to Louie: "About eleven o'clock his breathing became calm and slow, and his arms, which had been moved in a restless way at times, at length were folded on his breast. About twelve o'clock his breathing was still calmer, and slower, and his brow and lips were slightly cold and his eyes grew dim...." After the end came, John attempted to bring the entire family together for the funeral: "In a few days the snow will be falling on father's grave and one by one we will join him in his last rest, all our separating wanderings done forever."

In January 1886, a second daughter, Helen, was born to John and Louie. She was sick at birth, and, being an adoring father, Muir found that the child's frailty only added to his worries. Muir offered his brother and other members of the family jobs at the Martinez ranch overseeing the work he had been doing, but they couldn't leave their businesses for another year. Muir's ranch labor and his lowlander's ailments intensified. After accepting an offer to edit two volumes on the cycles of

Attempting to understand the love of the wild that afflicted her husband, Louie Muir accompanied John to Yosemite in the summer of 1884. Poking fun at his wife in a letter to their daughters (above), Muir sketched himself using a stick to prod Louie uphill. Following more in their father's footsteps, the two sisters, Wanda (on the left) and Helen, would flower into nature lovers capable of handling themselves in the wilderness.

JOHN MUIR: NATURE'S VISIONARY

Backed by coastal hills already stripped of trees, an 1860s sawmill on the Albion River in northern California characterizes what Muir called the "fierce storm of steel" that devoured much of the great western forests. Although the timber industry had once provided Muir with a living, in later life he came to deplore logging as an outrage against nature. "The outcries we hear against forest reservations come mostly from thieves who are wealthy and steal timber by wholesale," he bellowed in the August 1897 issue of Atlantic Monthly. *But Muir's passion did not quell rampant timbering; above, a turn-of-the-century logger in Humboldt County poses with a felled redwood.*

Boughs of western red cedar bask in the soft autumn light of Olympic National Forest. Overcome by the emerald bounty, Muir described the lush Washington rain forest as "untrodden woods where no axe has been lifted."

nature in California, Muir rented a room in a San Francisco hotel for peace and quiet, but the writing was uninspired. He had to go back to the font to get healed.

One day in 1888, while working in the orchard, Muir's Alaska friend, S. Hall Young came visiting. Muir dropped the basket of cherries he was holding and ran to greet him. Muir complained to Young of being lost in those orchards, saying that they obscured the view inward as well as outward. He was hoping that Young had come to rescue him from domestic slavery, but Young was on his way back from the far north.

Later, the two men sat on the porch of the house and talked about their exploits in Alaska. Muir had rediscovered America too late to see it truly wild; he could only read about it through the travel accounts of Catlin, Bartram, and Audubon. But Alaska offered a view not just of untrammeled places but of an aboriginal population only marginally changed. In the Aleutian, Eskimo, and Athapaskan villagers he had come to know, he saw fierce dignity, unconditional generosity toward their children, a deep knowledge of weather and place, a harmony with animals, and an uninhibited and spontaneous sense of festivity. He had never felt so at home among human beings.

John recalled the skin boats of the Eskimos on St. Lawrence Island with a tinge of envy and longing: "They had a few poles for the frame of the boat and skins to cover it, and for food a piece of walrus flesh which they ate raw. This, with a gun and a few odds and ends, was all their property, yet they seemed more confident of their ability to earn a living than most whites on their farms."

In Young's presence, Muir was ashamed of his domestic servitude and what he called "money-grubbing." Yet he could not stop being the Strentzel family's sacrificial lamb. After all, he had married into landed gentry when he was relatively penniless—not for the money but because he was disoriented and lonely. The Strentzels had given the house and original farm acreage to the newlyweds as a wedding present, and the Muirs had since remodeled the house. Now, Muir was a married, landed man himself and would have to play the role.

Young left and Muir stayed, badly disappointed. Between ranch work, child and wife care, Muir was writing his piece about Glacier Bay. As usual, his journal reveals a blend of despair and optimism: "Rain, wind, black weather with tedious monotony, but it matters not as far as my fields are concerned. In writing scenery I am in Alaska and the mind goes there with marvelous vividness. I see the mountains and the glaciers flowing down their gorges and broad shell-shaped hollows." Muir needed to take his own advice: "Everybody needs beauty as well as bread, places to play in and pray in, where Nature may heal and cheer and give strength to body and soul."

Muir would always be a wanderer. His feet were hungry for lateral moraines, boggy alpine meadows, ice cliffs, crevasses, and granite. Following Young's visit, something snapped in Muir, and, when the opportunity to go to the mountains was presented, he went. It was literally a matter of life and death. He could not hesitate any longer.

Lake Tahoe was his first stop on a botanizing trip with Charles Parry, then on to his beloved Mount Shasta with his best friend, William Keith. Much to his dismay, Muir found that during his seven-year retreat, the mountain world had been invaded by loggers, who had been given free rein. Muir decried the devastation of the forests surrounding Shasta, writing, "The glory is departing." The pair of friends continued on to Mount Hood, but Keith was ill and Muir had to content himself with daily strolls. On August 8, they joined six others to climb Mount Rainier.

To COME OUT OF HIS DOMESTIC RETREAT and find the money changers in the cathedral—the slopes of western mountains denuded, dug up, overgrazed, with shantytowns sprouting below them—was deeply shocking to Muir. But he was beginning to see with clarity that the American sensibility stood on an economic framework, one that applauded conquest, exploitation, pragmatism, industry, and the commercialization of every nook and cranny. Production and profitability were the goals; no aesthetic or spiritual element was mixed in. The need for nature's beauty was not seen as an imperative. Making a buck at any cost was.

Muir's dictum that everyone needs natural beauty was scoffed at by many as being frivolous, irrelevant, and unmanly. In the years to come he would have a tremendous fight on his hands, one that is still being fought.

During one of John's trips, Louie made a decision that showed how deeply she was concerned for her husband's well-being: She resolved that they should sell or lease large tracts of the ranch to help ease his workload. Everyone who had read his works wanted Muir to start writing full-time again, but that would not happen for a few more years. After all, it wasn't writing itself that Muir missed but rather living in the wild places about which he wrote.

In the spring of 1889, a meeting took place that would change not only Muir's life but the course of environmental history. While visiting San Francisco, Robert Underwood Johnson asked to meet Muir. Johnson was editor of *Century,* formerly *Scribner's Monthly.* Muir had contributed articles to the magazine before, and now

Working in the "scribble-den" in his Martinez home, Muir composed many of his most influential books and articles. Drowning in waves of paper, Muir was persuaded by his daughter Helen to tie red ribbons around finished manuscripts and file them in a fruit box.

Johnson had in mind a series Muir might write about the Sierra. Muir went to Johnson's hotel room in San Francisco looking bedraggled as usual with his long beard, tangled hair, and farmer's clothes. But as soon as he opened his mouth, the usual torrent of words flowed out in his charming Scottish burr. Johnson knew he had met his match. For his part, Muir immediately liked Johnson and even invited him on a trip to Yosemite.

They arrived on June 3. Beguiled by the valley's natural beauty, Johnson wandered around in awe, and Muir felt the instant refreshment that comes with mountain living. He visited old haunts and old friends but also saw how trampled by tourists the valley floor had become (around 5,000 visitors per year now came). He quickly organized a pack trip, and the two men rode up into the high country, sleeping on pine boughs in Tuolumne Meadows and camping the next night by the gorge.

Their faces reddened by campfire, Muir and Johnson mutually agreed that Yosemite needed more protection. Johnson recommended the formation of a national preserve, much like Yellowstone, that would keep the exploiters out but would allow those who simply wanted to see the place and sleep under the stars room to roam. But how could they make this dream happen? California politics were sticky; Johnson felt it would be better to go farther afield.

With this in mind, he asked Muir to write two articles for *Century*, extolling Yosemite's beauty. The readership of the magazine numbered 200,000, many of the best and brightest among them. Using Muir's written pieces as his springboard, Johnson would do the political footwork among his friends at home.

In August and September of 1890, Muir's two articles appeared, and he was suddenly back in form. His descriptions sang, creating an image for the mind's eye. Having accomplished this, Muir could then make a plea for the preservation of so beautiful a place. His appeal to the public was then, and always would be, based on spiritual grounds—who could not see that Yosemite was a song and a cathedral?

"All that is perishable is vanishing," Muir declared. As usual the work of writing about what he loved most was hard. To Johnson he wrote in an exasperated tone, "The love of Nature among Californians is desperately moderate; consuming enthusiasm almost wholly unknown."

With Muir's magazine pieces, the notion of a land ethic began to register in the public consciousness. Muir lobbied for "all the Yosemite fountains" to be included in the preserve, for no "other use than the use of beauty." The park should include the Tuolumne River, the central axis of the Sierra; the Big Tuolumne Meadows; the Tuolumne Canyon; and the Big Tree groves below the valley. The acceptance of these ideas required a broad shift in thinking about the living world and how to ensure its sanctity. "Treasures of the Yosemite" and "Features of the Proposed

Yosemite National Park" showed the public how the worth of a place could be measured not only by its monetary usefulness but by its own beauty and well-being. An outrageous concept had been put on the American table, one that Thoreau had already championed: "In wildness is the preservation of the world."

By the end of the spring of 1890 Muir was exhausted, and against doctor's orders he fled to his other beloved sanctuary, Alaska. By boat he traveled from Seattle to Port Townsend, Wrangell, Juneau, Douglas Island, and Glacier Bay. The farther north Muir got, the more his health improved. Along the way he examined trees, climbed mountains, and talked to villagers. He made a sled, which he pushed across the huge glacier named for him. He explored the confluence of the first of the glacier's seven tributaries and stopped for lunch: "To dine with a glacier on a sunny day is a glorious thing and makes common feasts of meat and wine ridiculous." Later, he camped on ice: "I am cozy and comfortable here resting in the midst of glorious icy scenery, though very tired. I made out to get a cup of tea by means of a few shavings and splinters whittled from the bottom board of my sled, and made a fire in a little can, a small campfire, the smallest I ever made.... One of my shoes is about worn out. I may have to put on a wooden sole. This day has been cloudless throughout, with lovely sunshine, a purple evening and morning."

When Muir returned to Martinez in September, he was renewed and refreshed, and the campaign for Yosemite was in full swing. On October 1, 1890, the bill that made Yosemite a national park passed. Johnson began urging Muir and his cronies in the Bay Area to form a watchdog association that would make sure Yosemite and California's other wild wonders were looked after. But nothing was done. Muir was absorbed in family concerns again.

On the last day of October, his father-in-law, Dr. John Strentzel, died in his sleep. Grief-stricken, the Muir family shifted into the big house to help take care of Mrs. Strentzel. Seventeen months later, Muir's brother David went bankrupt, and Muir had to go to Wisconsin to bail him out of trouble and bring him to Martinez. Despite these crises, John was no longer beset with fieldwork. As his literary career was relaunched, his relatives began taking over much of that work for him. More and more he committed himself to writing and lecturing for conservation.

In 1891 a law was passed with an attachment granting the President power to create "forest preserves." At the urging of the Secretary of the Interior John Noble

President William Henry Harrison put more than 13 million acres of wildlands into preserves, including a 200-mile-long, 4-million-acre ridgetop tract in the southern Sierra. It was a major conservation victory, one that was especially gratifying to Muir. But the fight to preserve more "sacred groves" continued: Muir was still trying to include Kings Canyon in Sequoia National Park.

In the midst of these battles, the old idea of forming a watchdog association finally took hold. On May 28, 1892, two Berkeley professors, one a German philologist and the other an English teacher, assembled a small group at the office of a San Francisco attorney, Warren Olney, who was also an ardent amateur mountaineer. The group had gathered to form "a Sierra Club." By June 4, the Sierra Club's articles of incorporation had been signed by 27 men and John Muir made president. He was thrilled with the prospect of the new club. His lonely love affair with the natural world now included other mountain lovers, among them some of his closest friends: William Keith, J.B. McChesney, Galen Clark, Joseph Le Conte, Adolph Sutro, and even his old employer, the now divorced James Hutchings.

Almost immediately the power of the organization was tested. The Caminetti bill was introduced to reduce the size of Yosemite. It passed the Senate, but as it was being presented to the House, Muir and the others in the Sierra Club besieged representatives and the press with their objections. The bill was tabled for that session and eventually defeated. From that day on, the idea of conserving land for no other use than to observe and ponder its beauty established a grassroots footing that became one of the most powerful political tools in the country. Again and again the club, representing those with a deep love of unspoiled nature, made hard charges against public apathy and corporate and political hostility. Muir's initial battle to save trees ended up preserving more, and how could it not? A vision of the unity that Muir felt and saw everywhere was now entering the public imagination. So was the legend of John Muir.

His life of passion and solitude in the High Sierra had been translated into a campaign to turn other people's minds and hearts away from the plodding, workaday world to a realization of the healing spirituality of the wilderness. Even in Muir's darkest times—through childhood beatings, near-death experiences, bouts of malaria, and near-starvation—Muir had pushed against the grain of industrial America. He stood up in each new day open-armed, receptive, healed and rehealed by the mountain wall, waterfall, windstorm, tree trunk, ouzel, raindrop, bee pasture, and glacier. He was content to be "a flake of grass through which light passes," content to be a small part of nature's reality. At the same time, he had become a political warrior, fighting not for himself but for voiceless mountains, animals, and trees.

The Martinez ranch had become a salon of sorts, as many well-known people

Although Muir took great comfort in his life with his wife, Louie, and their daughters, Wanda (left) and Helen, he could never really reconcile himself to the wearisome task of managing his father-in-law's farm outside the northern California town of Martinez.

came to visit. Muir and Louie had successfully shifted the workload to others, and at age 55, between campaigns to preserve tracts of land, he allowed himself to relax. He often visited Keith's studio on Montgomery Street along with writer Charles Lummis, poets Edward Taylor and Charles Keeler, and Joseph Worcester, a clergyman with the mystical Swedenborgian church.

In May 1893, the group of friends impulsively decided to go to Europe together. Keith went first, and Muir hopscotched across the country behind him, never quite catching up. In New York, Robert Underwood Johnson diverted Muir

I am hopelessly and forever a mountaineer ...and I care to live only to entice people to look at Nature's loveliness.

~JM

Muir (center) frequently explored the wilderness with other ardent conservationists. Here, he takes a rest with his good friend, artist William Keith (on left), and an unidentified young man.

JOHN MUIR: NATURE'S VISIONARY

A highlight of Muir's 1888 foray into the Pacific Northwest was the opportunity to explore the "bulk and majesty" of Mount Rainier, reflected above. "I did not mean to climb it," Muir wrote later, almost as if he were ashamed of the deed, "but got excited and soon was on top." At left, western pasqueflowers and lupine carpet a meadow on the flank of Naches Peak in Mount Rainier National Park. Muir's tireless efforts to preserve the peak finally paid off in 1899, when President McKinley created the national park.

In a prelude to the last great battle of his conservation career, Muir guided a Sierra Club outing through Yosemite's Hetch Hetchy Valley in 1909. With Muir as one of its founding fathers, the club became a prototype for the myriad environmental organizations that sprouted later in the 20th century.

into a month-long series of meetings and parties, where he met Mark Twain, Rudyard Kipling, John Burroughs, and Nikola Tesla, among many others. He also made the requisite trip to the Massachusetts village of Concord to visit the graves of his friend Ralph Waldo Emerson and Henry David Thoreau.

In the meantime, Keith and his wife sailed for Europe. Muir was still embroiled in social visits to botanists and paleontologists in New York City and sailed for Liverpool on June 26, three weeks later than Keith. They never did catch up with each other.

From the west coast of England Muir made his way to his childhood home in Dunbar, Scotland. He had not revisited it since he left as a boy. The house his family had lived in had been converted into the Lorne Temperance Hotel. But he could still stroll around the crumbling castle and walk the rocky coast. He wrote to his daughter Wanda, "The waves made…grand songs, the same old songs they sang to me in my childhood, and I seemed a boy again.…"

The tour continued. In Switzerland Muir stood before the "huge savage pyramid" of the Matterhorn but chose to climb a smaller mountain. He complained that his French accent was so bad even the dogs couldn't understand him. He continued through the Alps to Lake Como, down through northern Italy, and back to London, Edinburgh, and Dunbar again, visiting friends and relatives. On his way home, a telegram from Louie prompted him to go to Washington, D.C., and lobby for Yosemite with the new Secretary of the Interior, Hoke Smith.

It was mid-October by the time Muir returned home, and he immediately went to work shaping and organizing his essays for *The Mountains of California*, which was published in 1894. The book was a hit and galvanized the public into continued efforts to preserve the nation's remaining watershed forests.

IN JUNE 1896 MUIR HAD A SUDDEN SENSE that all was not well with his aging mother, Ann, then living with two of her daughters in Portage, Wisconsin. Trusting his instinct, Muir immediately took a train east, wiring ahead to his brothers and sisters to join him. Sister Mary complied, and the two arrived to find their mother gravely ill. Within two weeks, she was gone.

At about this time a federal commission had been appointed to recommend a national forestry policy for the preservation and governance of forested lands. Though asked to be a member, Muir declined but agreed to serve as an adviser. Among the commissioners was Gifford Pinchot, a young man who had just completed forestry studies in Germany and had been working to preserve trees in the Adirondacks. He and other commission members hoped to convince lawmakers to establish a National Forestry Commission, which would not only preserve trees but also manage some tracts for sustained yields. Pinchot was ambitious, and that ambition would darken Muir's conservation efforts in the future.

After a long Forestry Commission tour, which took in the forests of the Black Hills, the Bighorn and Bitterroot Mountains, and Washington and Oregon, as well as the redwoods of California and the oaks of the Grand Canyon, a report was made. Muir was one of its contributors. While Muir and his friends were preservationists, Pinchot had a multiple-use approach to the forests. This philosophical rift would widen later.

JOHN MUIR: NATURE'S VISIONARY

Drifting without human charts through light and dark, calm and storm, I have come to so glorious an ocean.

~JM

Pounding the rugged cliffs of the Oregon coast, the Pacific never failed to inspire Muir with its "grand, savage harmony."

Finally, a recommendation was made to President Cleveland in 1897. He responded favorably, issuing an Executive Order that set aside thirteen new forest reserves in eight western states. In total, more than 21 million acres were protected by the order.

The western lumbermen, miners, and many of the ranchers and senators were furious, and Muir was immediately enlisted to go to war with his pen, which he did. For the *Atlantic Monthly,* he wrote "The American Forests," the first sentence of which alone must have caused outrage: "The American forests, however slighted by man, must surely have been a great delight to God; for they were the best he ever planted. The whole continent was a garden, and from the beginning it seemed favored above all the other wild parks and gardens of the globe."

Rhapsody turned to elegy and elegy to polemic in this smoldering essay, as Muir described the entire continent's forests. He also outlined his own plan for preservation and ended with this: "Any fool can destroy trees. They cannot run away; and if they could, they would still be destroyed—chased and hunted down as long as fun or a dollar could be got out of their bark hides, branching horns, or magnificent bole backbones."

Not long after, Muir aired his grievances against Gifford Pinchot openly in the lobby of a Seattle hotel. Though Pinchot had acknowledged the damage sheep had done to mountain lands, he subsequently made a statement to the papers that overgrazing did little harm to forest reserves. Muir confronted him: "Are you correctly quoted here?" he asked Pinchot, who answered that he was. "Then if that is the case, I don't want anything more to do with you."

For the first time, John Muir tasted the bitterness of the conservation battles that were to come. ▪

Gliding high above Puget Sound fog, Mount Rainier beckons climbers from all around the globe. Many of them overnight at 10,000-foot Camp Muir, scaling the rest of the peak at dawn. Muir climbed the peak—virtually without equipment—in 1888 at the age of 50.

Three generations of John Muir's descendants—grandson John Hanna (left), great-grandson Bill Hanna(middle), and great-great-grandson Michael Hanna—take a break from chores at their northern California vineyard, where they continue a century-long, family tradition of fruit farming.

CHAPTER SIX

Wandering to the End

John Muir
at about seventy

Forty-one years after John Muir's first summer in the Sierra, he began piecing together his notes and newspaper and magazine articles to make his books. His discipline at the writing table occurred in direct proportion to the debilitations of his body; his frostbitten foot didn't work well and his respiratory ailments were more frequent. The harder it was for him to climb mountains, the easier it became, apparently, to stay home and write. But containing the rapture and exultation in something as paltry as words would forever feel like an impossibility, if not a tiresome chore. For Muir, those rattling words were so much easier to speak than to write. Yet the public clamored for more, and so he obliged them and wrote.

It had never been celebrity that drove Muir to the writing life but rather an evangelistic urge. Muir had "ouzel tales to tell," and he took it upon himself to address the nation on behalf of those who were languageless—all the wild places and beings—first to tell of their existence and their primal beauty and then to attempt to keep their beauty from being destroyed.

By the time *The Mountains of California* arrived in bookstores, Muir was 56 years old, and the stories he recounted—climbing Mount Ritter, walking across the Central Valley, riding a tree during a windstorm, celebrating a water ouzel—were all experiences from his early years of seclusion in the mountains. Those precious, contemplative years were monastic compared to the last, peripatetic decade and to the half of his life when he spun around and around the country and the world. For every few days on a mountain or glacier or in a forest, he had spent many more days visiting dignitaries, politicians, scholars, and friends, as if in an effort to stave off the great loneliness that would come with the death of many of his loved ones and his own inevitable passing.

Between 1897 and 1914, Muir's life took on an almost frantic pace, with his time chopped up into increasingly smaller units. His days were filled with politics, lecturing, book writing, and spending time with his two daughters and Louie. But the short forays into the wilderness continued: He visited the Selkirk and Rocky Mountains and southeastern Alaska to study trees; he went to Mount Shasta and Mount Scott then crossed the country to the East Coast to visit friends.

The next year Muir accepted an invitation to return to Alaska with the 1899 Harriman Alaska Expedition, orchestrated by railroad magnate E.H. Harriman. Along with Harriman's wife and several family members, the expedition included a distinguished list of scientists—naturalist John B. Burroughs, geologist Henry Gannett, and biologist C. Hart Merriam. It was Muir, though, who had had firsthand experience of the regions for which they were headed.

They sailed from Seattle in May with 126 people aboard the *George W. Elder*. It was a lively group, and Harriman spared no expense. Muir's cabinmate was the Berkeley poet Charles Keeler. In the evenings there were sumptuous meals, music, poetry readings, and storytelling—mostly Muir's.

Burroughs and Muir, distant friends of long standing, spent the trip engaged in "whimsical, growling banter" and cruel taunts. Burroughs was anything but an adventurous traveler, and Muir, whom Burroughs had nicknamed "Cold Storage Muir," wanted things wilder, colder, icier, and more northern. For his part, Muir let his boyish humor fly in teasing J.B., particularly when he tried to steal off the boat before it reached the Bering Sea. At the same time, though, he worried about the older man's ill health and sent others to Burroughs's cabin to make sure that he was all right.

Along the way, Muir and Harriman developed an unexpectedly strong friendship. No two men could have been more opposite. Harriman was reportedly cold and detached, while Muir was passionate and disheveled. Later, Harriman would be instrumental in helping Muir preserve Yosemite Valley.

Despite his unremitting wanderlust, Muir was devoted to his family. After the death of his wife, Louie, in 1905, Muir drew closer to his daughters and their numerous children, never tiring of their romps around the family farm in Martinez. Here, he plays with his young grandson Strentzel Hanna.

President Teddy Roosevelt (opposite) and Muir pose at Glacier Point, having had a "bully" time during their 1903 camping trip in Yosemite. In 1909, Muir guided another President, William Howard Taft, and a cadre of luminaries through Yosemite. The party paused for a picture as they passed through a giant sequoia.

As the ship cruised along the coast of the Alaska Panhandle, Muir looked out longingly at the small villages and at the Inuit hunters who came alongside in their umiaks—animal-hide boats big enough to carry several families as well as cargo. "Fifteen to thirty persons in each, beside babies and dogs, provisions, skiis, etc.—a merry gypsy crowd," Muir wrote.

At St. Lawrence Island the boat stopped to let off botanists, geologists, and biologists at various places. The scientists carried out their studies in the water, under trees, on the ice: "Got possession of a few goslings and plants and sight of three polar bears, which turned out after a hot pursuit to be swans! In the evening we sailed for St. Matthew Island."

It didn't matter how many times Muir had been to Alaska, nothing jaded his eye to its magnificence. On St. Matthew he found, "The ground was everywhere flowery, though said to be less so than at the two other landings. Lupine, Astragalus, Oxytropis, charming Primula, Stellaria, mats of pink ball, shrubby Chamaecistus, Silene, Arnica, Tussilago, Anemone, viola, dwarf willow, pink Andromeda, very fine Claytonia, etc. Great banks of snow indicate violent winds on dusty snow; some banks seem perpetual, have terminal moraines and a sort of glacial motion; some reach sea-level…," he wrote. Farther north, he spent days clambering over icebergs and glaciers in his usual state of delight. If the boat had left him there, he would have been glad, but he had a foot in two worlds and some string always pulled him back to the "civilized" one.

John Muir would live only 14 years into the 20th century, and most of those years he spent writing and working for the preservation of forests and parks. He was 63 years old when President McKinley was shot and Teddy Roosevelt became President, and for a while there was great optimism among the mountain lovers. That unexpected historical twist moved conservation to the first order of business in Washington, D.C.

"We are not building this country of ours for a day. It is to last through the ages," Roosevelt proclaimed. Roosevelt had come to the outdoor life as a refuge from childhood sickness. He was asthmatic and his parents made him play outside for his health. Lured by natural history books, hunting trips, and a college summer spent in the Maine woods, he made the natural world his calling. He was born into American aristocracy and could have built any sort of life for himself. In 1884, after his young wife and his mother died on the same day, Teddy fled to the West. In the badlands of the Dakota Territory, he bought a ranch, and in those open spaces, amid the cowboy life, he found solace.

As President, Roosevelt requested a meeting with Muir to help understand the real needs of the western wildernesses. Muir had a European trip planned with his old friend Charles Sargent and Sargent's son. He hesitated at the idea of changing the trip in order to take T.R. into Yosemite. But when Roosevelt sent Muir a personal message that said, "I do not want anyone with me but you, and I want to drop politics absolutely for four days, and just be out in the open with you," Muir hesitated no longer.

From the valley floor they packed supplies on the backs of a few mules, hired a cook, and rode up into the mountains with two rangers as Secret Service men. They camped without tents under the giant sequoias of the Mariposa Grove, grilled steaks over an open fire, and spoke about what they knew and loved. Roosevelt talked of bear, antelope, bison, and the sinuous Missouri, and identified the flutelike song in the woods as that of a hermit thrush, a bird Muir didn't know. Muir rhapsodized about the purple sap of the giant sequoia and the wild gardens of pine, fir, spruce, cedar, and sequoia. As the campfire died down, Muir and the President unrolled their blankets on beds Muir had improvised, as he frequently did, from spruce and pine boughs. A hood of stars arched over the two friends, who had come from opposite ends of the social spectrum—one a penniless wanderer for much of his youth, the other pampered and privileged but cut down by grief. Both had sought out the natural world, free for the taking.

At the end of the four days a storm dumped four inches of cold snow on top of their sleeping bags. To this, Roosevelt crowed, "This is bullier yet!" Muir would recall it as one of the best times he had ever spent with anyone in the mountains. But the trip proved much more far-reaching in its ultimate effect. It had convinced the President just how essential was the return of Yosemite Valley to federal hands, if further depredations were to be stopped. "No small part of the prosperity of California…depends upon the preservation of her water supply; and the water supply cannot be preserved unless the forests are preserved as well…." By the end of his tenure, President Roosevelt was responsible for adding to Yosemite National Park, as well as creating five other national parks and setting aside 55 wildlife preserves and 150 national forests.

From Yosemite, Muir immediately left for the East to begin his postponed journey with Charles Sargent to Europe and Asia. The European travel, with its city visits and museums, fatigued him, and it wasn't until they reached Russia that Muir perked up. While the others slept, John leaned out the train window, soaking up the scent and sight of the grainfields of the Volga Valley and the great forests of "indomitable birch" in Siberia.

In Manchuria, Muir became deathly ill from bad food. He'd had enough of people, and, when he was able to get up again, he parted ways with the Sargents and continued on alone to India. In the hill stations of Darjiling and Simla he basked in the sight of the Himalaya towering in the north. In Egypt, he traveled up the Nile on a steamer. Finally, he began the long trip home, heading east and stopping in the Blue Mountains of Australia, then continuing on to admire the alpine flora of New Zealand, where he reported that he was "beginning botany all over again."

From the South Pacific, he traveled to the Philippines and Japan and walked among the sacred gardens of a Shinto shrine. By the time he again saw San Francisco Bay, he had been absent from home for a year.

D URING THE WINTER OF 1905, John Muir campaigned hard for the recession of Yosemite Valley into federal hands. He made nine trips in two months to Sacramento to testify before committees of the state legislature. Then, at the end of February, the recession bill passed both houses of the legislature. But the battle was only half won. The U.S. House and Senate in Washington had to accept the receded grant, and more fights ensued. Muir asked Harriman for help and got it, but there were more delays. Finally, after years of political infighting—which Muir recognized as the embroilments of egos and self-interests—Congress passed a bill in June 1906 making Yosemite Valley a part of Yosemite National Park.

Family problems soon absorbed Muir's attention. His beloved younger daughter, Helen, whose health had been fragile since birth, came down with another bout of pneumonia. Hoping to allay her chronic respiratory problems, John and his older daughter, Wanda, took Helen to a ranch near Willcox, Arizona. A man of tall trees and alpine meadows, Muir found he could love the arid mountains and grasslands of Arizona as well his Sierra aeries. Helen thrived in her new surroundings—a hacienda, open country, and lots of sun—but an urgent telegram from Louie asked John and Wanda to come home. Fifty-seven years old, Louie had been diagnosed with lung cancer and had very little time to live.

JOHN MUIR: NATURE'S VISIONARY

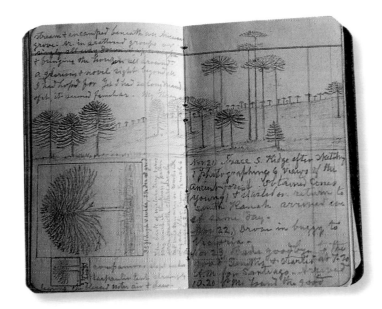

Coconut palms bow to the relentless bluster of a Hawaiian storm. Although most often associated with redwoods, Muir had a lifelong fascination with trees of all kinds. "We all travel the milky way together, trees and men," he once wrote. "One of the greatest of the great tree days of my lucky life," Muir gushed in his journal (left), when he first encountered a baobab tree in the African bush. On his 1911 trip to South America, Muir sketched the Araucaria imbricata (above), a coniferous tree indigenous to southern Chile.

When Louie Strentzel Muir died on August 6, 1905, John was devastated. He had begun his adult life as a wanderer, but with Louie he had found an emotional and terrestrial tie on the family farm that complemented his spiritual tie to the mountains. Though he was absent from the Martinez ranch and from Louie often, a strong sense of support and concern bound them tightly together. She had learned that his love could be won only by letting him go his own wild way. In return he was loyal and grateful, an adoring father and husband, though an unwilling householder. She had been his critic, editor, and helpmate, but she could never share his mountain joy. Now, ironically, the feet that had taken him thousands of miles would hardly move. He was lost, and it would be almost six years before he traveled far from home again.

The earthquake and fire that ravaged much of San Francisco in April 1906 must have seemed like yet more upheaval in Muir's life. Much of the next year was spent with his daughters, particularly with Helen in Adamana, Arizona. In the desert there, Muir discovered thousands of fossilized trees and was so fascinated by the relics and so horrified by their destruction at the hands of "money-grubbers" that he helped bring into being the 1906 formation of the Petrified Forest National Monument, signed by his old camping friend, Teddy Roosevelt.

Helen's health fluctuated. It was probably never very good, and before antibiotics there was no help for pneumonia; only those who were strong survived. She did survive but had to be moved between various Arizona ranches and the family home in Martinez. In the meantime, Wanda married a civil engineer from Berkeley, and they took over the old adobe on the Martinez ranch.

Muir continued to feel lost without Louie, but he turned to his daughters for companionship. They were as devoted to him as he was to them, and though they weren't mountain raised, they had some of Muir's physical toughness. They could ride a horse, drive a six-horse team, pitch in with ranch chores, and hold their own in debates during the battles to save Yosemite.

In June and July of 1907, Muir, accompanied by Wanda, went on his usual month-long trip to Yosemite and Hetch Hetchy with the Sierra Club. The fight to save Hetch Hetchy from being dammed for a municipal water supply for San Francisco was heating up. Much to his dismay, Muir discovered the mentality of most "flatlanders" so ingrained that the natural abundance and diversity of the world, in this case, Hetch Hetchy—the Grand Canyon of the Tuolumne, a second Yosemite—were unimaginable and its wonders not worth saving: "Yosemite is so wonderful that we are apt to regard it as an exceptional creation, the only valley of its kind in the world; but Nature is not so poor as to have only one of anything. Several other yosemites have been discovered in the Sierra...."

"I may yet become a proper cultivated plant," Muir wrote in 1872, "cease my wild wanderings…." But he never did. His twilight years included travels to Europe, Asia, Africa, South America, and Australia (above), where a skiff proved the most efficient means for his party of naturalists to see local flora and fauna.

Even his most elegant descriptions fell on deaf ears. He compared the two valleys: rounded domes and rock walls; the gardens of wildflowers with their "abundance of showy and fragrant herbaceous plants"; and the waterfalls—particularly Hetch Hetchy's Tueeulala, with its "silvery scarf burning with irised sun-fire," its waters of "combed silk," and the wide bottom of the falls "composed of yet finer tissues…air, water and sunlight woven into stuff that spirits might wear."

A few months later in October, with the fight still on, Muir camped for a week in Hetch Hetchy with William Keith, who had made many drawings and paintings

W
ildness so godful,
cosmic, primeval, bestows
a new sense of earth's
beauty and size.

~ JM

*Muir's words, above, still
echo the magnificence of the
Grand Canyon, as winter
and sunrise lighten the
canyon rims.*

Coda to a desert thunderstorm, a rainbow (right) arcs over the barren terrain of Petrified Forest National Park. With a petrified log as his writing desk, Muir (above) took notes on one of his forays there during his 1905-1906 stay in the desert. Helen Muir's respiratory ailments prompted the temporary move to arid northern Arizona, where her father discovered, to his surprise, that deserts could be just as beguiling as forests, mountains, or marshlands.

Muir conceded in this 1908 letter that the battle to save the handsome Hetch Hetchy Valley in Yosemite National Park from flooding was all but lost. "Dam Hetch-Hetchy!" Muir thundered. "As well dam for water-tanks the people's cathedrals and churches."

there in the past and continued to do so. Combining words and pictures to fight for the preservation of the wilderness had been a tried and true strategy with Muir and Keith, but now it proved ineffective against the meaner, more venal politics of the new century. The fight to save the Grand Canyon of the Tuolumne, the wild part of the park that Muir claimed was even more beautiful than Yosemite Valley, signaled the end of Muir's hold on the public imagination. The art of saving land was becoming the art of compromise; the moneylenders were already in the temple, and it was now impossible to have them removed.

MUIR MISTAKENLY THOUGHT he could save Hetch Hetchy because of its obscurity and inaccessibility: Give Yosemite Valley to the "soft, succulent" city dwellers, and save the wilder parts of the Yosemite and Tuolumne watersheds. Nothing worked. Former allies became actual enemies. Everything that Muir stood for— awakened mind and awakened heart; awareness and enthusiasm for each day as it unfolded; a joie de vivre unupholstered by money, false fronts, alcohol, or celebrity; quiet celebrations of life made possible by the practice of compassion, generosity, self-discipline, and patience—all this was ignored, berated, and trivialized. Many of those who knew of Muir dismissed him as romantic, unmanly, unwashed, irrational, impractical, and childish.

Muir wrote a letter on his birthday, April 21, 1908, pleading with President Roosevelt: "Hetch-Hetchy is not a meadow: it is a Yosemite Valley…. These sacred mountain temples are the holiest ground that the heart of man has consecrated, and it behooves us all faithfully to do our part in seeing that our wild mountain parks are passed on unspoiled to those who come after us, for they are national properties in which every man has a right and interest…. P.S. Oh for a tranquil camp hour with you like those beneath the sequoias in memorable 1903!"

His pleas did no good. Roosevelt had become convinced, somehow, that the national interests—and the conservation of natural resources—were part of a greater problem of "national efficiency, the patriotic duty of insuring the safety and continuance of the nation." In other words, beauty was of little use and the exploitation of the natural world was king. No grand canyon could compare. Muir's words were magic no more. Muir's writing had grown tired because he was tired in his long stay in the rooms of so-called "civilization." Both he and Roosevelt had been away from the mountains and the untamed life too long.

In the midst of battle, Muir discovered too late that he had enemies. William Kent, who had donated a grove of redwoods in Muir's name, voted to dam Hetch Hetchy. But far worse, his old rival Gifford Pinchot, who had become the first chief of the Forest Service, had personally advised a San Francisco city official in May 1906 to "make provision for a water supply from the Yosemite National Park."

The betrayal was complete. Hetch Hetchy was doomed. (A few years later, on the east side of the Sierra, the Owens Valley was drained of its water.) "These temple destroyers, devotees of ravaging commercialism, seem to have a perfect contempt for Nature, and instead of lifting their eyes to the mountains, lift them to dams and town skyscrapers," Muir lamented. Heartbroken, in bad health, ever longing for mountain joys and tranquillity, Muir was a beaten man. Even the Sierra Club members found themselves divided on this and other issues—between pure preservation, as put forward by "spiritual lobbyists" like Muir, and Pinchot's utilitarian "wise-use" policies, which ultimately bowed to commercial interests.

The loss of Hetch Hetchy began the slow undoing of John Muir. He had always hated politics, yet he had come down from the mountains and gone headlong into the fray. Reclusive, shy, uninterested in the self-serving struggles of human beings, he nevertheless had no choice but to speak out if he wanted to save his kingdom from its spoilers. That was the central irony of his life. After the loss of Hetch Hetchy, his heartbreak had extended far beyond the loss of Louie; now his heart's home had been defiled.

When the young John Muir had first dared to dream of travel and botanizing expeditions to faraway places, he had dreamed of going to South America, where he could paddle dugout canoes down the Amazon, explore the alpine flora of the Andes, and the vegetation of the Chilean deserts. His derailment to the Sierra in 1868, which was only to have lasted a few months, had already lasted 43 years. In 1911, after his daughter Helen regained her health and married, and he had published his early memoir, *My First Summer in the Sierra,* Muir at last took the long-awaited trip to South America. His best friend, William Keith, had just died, and he wrote, "I wonder if leaves feel lonely when they see their neighbors falling." Sad and estray, he was still eager for new adventures: "The world's big and I want to have a good look at it before it gets dark," he wrote. When he set sail for South America on August 11, 1911, he was 74.

He called the Amazon Basin through which he soon sailed a "rubbery wilderness," and he delighted in the massed life of trees, grasses, shrubs, insects, snakes, birds, and people. At one point he crawled on hands and knees under long vines searching for *Victoria regia,* a nymphaeaceous plant with a huge white blossom and spreading leaves.

Muir had already passed away when Hetch Hetchy was clear-cut, as shown in this historic photograph. The timbering was a prelude to construction of the controversial O'Shaughnessy Dam, still standing today. Many of Muir's friends speculated that his death was accelerated by the looming destruction of the High Sierra wonder.

Later, he accompanied some lumbermen he met on a boat sailing south to Santos to see the *Araucaria braziliana*—a conifer resembling a pine—in the midst of a "primeval forest" with "crowns like umbrella tops rising above each other.... Tree ferns fifteen to twenty feet high, fronds five feet long."

From Buenos Aires he went by buggy then horseback into a forest where he found a ridge lined with *Araucaria imbricata*, the monkey-puzzle tree, and much to his surprise, everywhere he went he was known, feted, and taken care of.

JOHN MUIR: NATURE'S VISIONARY

*"The clearest way into the Universe is through a forest wilderness,"
Muir wrote during an 1890 trip to Alaska. Throughout his lifetime,
he never ceased marveling at trees and their changing demeanor
through the changing seasons. At left, flowering dogwoods in
Kentucky hail the advent of spring. Above, snow-laden pines huddle
against the winter chill in Mount Rainier National Park.*

In December Muir sailed for Africa. He hadn't even told his daughters that he planned to visit that continent for fear that they would prevent him from going. He was a tramp again. "No sound of wind save a low whispering from small waves brushing the ship's side, and the low heart beats of the engines….The ship glides smoothly like a star."

On Christmas Eve, aboard the small steamer he and the others, a bit homesick, sang Christmas carols. He arrived in Cape Town in mid-January. Muir's whole purpose in going to Africa was to see the baobab trees. After staying at Victoria Falls in what was then Rhodesia, he enlisted the help of a young child and followed him into the hills to a grove of baobabs. "Kings may be blest but I am glorious! Wandered about in the woods that fringe the Falls, dripping with spray, and through the Baobab woods…. It is easily recognized by its skin-like bark, and its massive trunk and branches. The bark…looks like leather, or the skin of a hippopotamus…," he wrote to his daughter Helen.

After more than seven months of wandering, river gliding, tree hunting, waterfall soaking, Muir returned home. In March 1912, on arriving in New York, he immediately set to work proofreading galleys for his autobiography and a collection of essays called *The Yosemite*. He attended John Burroughs's birthday party on April 3 then left for California.

At home Muir succumbed to fatigue and caught a cold that turned to bronchitis. The Hetch Hetchy controversy was still going on, because the hearings had been continually postponed. President Taft, who had succeeded Roosevelt, was replaced in turn by Woodrow Wilson, who appointed Frank Lane, formerly the city attorney for San Francisco, as his secretary of the interior. Despite continued protests, it seemed that Hetch Hetchy's fate was sealed. Unwilling to give up, Muir kept a flow of letters and telegrams going to Washington.

Still at his desk every morning, he worked on the notes of his wanderings from Alaska to the Amazon. In July his daughter Helen gave birth to a second son, named Stanley, and John went south to see his new grandson. Returning more tired than ever, he signed a contract for *Travels in Alaska* and played with his grandsons, Wanda's children, who lived in the family compound. His daily delight was taking them for walks through the orchards, as he had his own children.

In August Muir's longtime friend John "Daddy" Swett died. A few months earlier they had both been given honorary degrees by the University of California at Berkeley. Now Swett was gone, Hetch Hetchy was to be dammed, and there was nothing left for John Muir to do except get his own affairs in order.

During the intense autumn heat of California, Mrs. Harriman insisted that John come to their Island Park Ranch in Idaho for a short vacation. Once there, he felt

Four years after Muir's death, the University of Wisconsin honored one of its most celebrated students by dedicating Muir Knoll, overlooking Lake Mendota. Muir's passion for botany was sparked by a flowering campus locust.

his boyish enthusiasms well up again and went for walks along "the clear, shimmering, whispering, slow-gliding river." A late night thunderstorm woke him with a "grand display of zigzag, intensely vivid and very near lightning, with keen crashes, grand trailing rain tresses."

By November the Hetch Hetchy problem was still being debated, and, ever the optimist, Muir wrote to Helen, "The H.H. question will probably be decided in the first week of December next and I still think we will win. Anyhow I'll be relieved when it's settled, for it's killing me."

When World War I broke out, Muir was completely disheartened by the human capacity for brutality to other humans; the callousness that had allowed Hetch Hetchy to be lost seemed to be endemic. That winter Muir's respiratory infection got worse. He was living in his big Victorian house with Ah Fong, the Chinese housekeeper who had been with the family for years. The house hadn't been touched since Louie died, but now carpenters were hired to fix it up.

Muir longed to see his daughter Helen and continually sent her boxes of fruit and clippings of shrubs from the ranch. Finally, he wrote to her as Christmas approached: "There is no one in the old house but myself. If I could only have you and Wanda as in the auld lang syne, it would be lovely. But such backward thoughts are all in vain…. I have got electric light now in the house and everything has been put in comparative order."

Finally, he went to see Helen and her family at their ranch outside Daggett, California, in the Mojave Desert, making sure he brought the manuscript of his Alaska book with him. The desert was cold, and his health worsened. Still, he and his daughter went for a walk, botanizing as they went, greeting every plant. By nightfall, pneumonia had come on, and he staggered when he tried to get up. He was taken by train to the California Hospital in Los Angeles. Wanda hurried to his bedside, which was even then covered with manuscript pages.

Muir had always danced between the tiniest detail and the most panoramic view. He was a man on whom nothing was lost. Some time earlier he had written, "This grand show is eternal. It is always sunrise somewhere; the dew is never all dried at once; a shower is forever falling; vapor is ever rising. Eternal sunrise, eternal sunset, eternal dawn and gloaming, on sea and continents and islands, each in its turn, as the round earth rolls."

On Christmas Eve, when for a moment neither daughter nor nurse was in the room, John Muir took his last breath. Alone and at peace but in love with every day and every inch of the vast world he had seen, as well as "the touch of invisible things," he wandered quietly over the ridge.

In one of his last "Sierra Fragments" he wrote, "How interesting it would be to keep close beside an ouzel all his life, and be present at his death-bed! Surely there would be no gloom, no pain. I fancy he would vanish like a flower, or a foam-bell at the foot of a waterfall." In speaking of his favorite bird, "the mountain streams' own darling, the humming-bird of blooming waters," whose home was in the high mountains, John Muir had described his own life and his passing. ■

Liz Hanna, great-great-granddaughter of John and Louie Strentzel Muir, tends a marker in the family cemetery in Martinez, California. Like many of Muir's descendants, she feels a special link to the past and keeps the legacy alive with her own environmental activism.

By 1902, when Muir posed for this portrait in Sequoia National Park, his status as nature's most eloquent advocate was well established.

A Shared Vision

WHEN JOHN MUIR CAME DOWN from the mountains in the 1870s to tell the world about his Sierra house and sequoia cathedral, he declared that "every feature of Nature's big face is beautiful,—height, hollow, wrinkle, furrow, and line...." Determined to do what he could to stop the depredation of these mountains and valleys, he was flying in the face of 19th-century values, which held that expansion, industry, human dominance, and profit constituted the primary good. In proclaiming that the wild Earth held all the answers, Muir invited contempt. Instead of conquering nature, he gave himself to it in surrender. Instead of cultivating the Edenic garden with ideals of a perfection that are forever unattainable, he offered the aesthetics of the wild—unruly, weed-choked, storm-battered, droughty, and ephemeral.

The more tourists and scientists visited and then left his mountain fastness, the more tenaciously he stayed, becoming "native to the place," believing that intimacy, observation, and awareness, not merely scholarship, are paths to knowledge. He believed in the intrinsic wholeness of the natural world and the essential human link to and perception of it. He spoke of wholes within wholes, millions of tiny universes—raindrops and drainages and cordilleras, macro and micro—all jostling together, all seething, all modulating into one spinning unity.

Muir had not planned a career in writing or conservation politics, had not foreseen that he would be instrumental in preserving Yosemite Valley and other wildlands or in founding the Sierra Club. In coming down from the mountains, he knew only that his sacred duty was to teach people to see.

For the next 20 years Muir mesmerized audiences with his rhapsodies of mountain joy and later tried to persuade the monied and powerful to act in the interest of preserving the trees, the Douglas squirrels, the water ouzels, the waterfalls, the glaciers, mountains, meadows, and lowland bee-pastures. Hawkeyed, beauty-haunted, and rail thin, he served as the intermediary between heaven and Earth. His God was everywhere, in everything; nothing he did on or off the mountains could have come into being without a spiritual impetus, and his sense of divinity was so deep and far-reaching as to encompass the living and nonliving—both flesh and rock. To John Muir, a sacred thread ran through all things.

The rapture Muir felt as he sauntered and studied did not easily adjust itself to the compression chamber of prose. Nevertheless, his highly embellished, exultant writing changed the way people thought about the natural world. The essays in *The Mountains of California* were assembled first and published in 1894, while his autobiography, *The Story of My Boyhood and*

Youth, was not pieced together until 1911. Three years later, he was working on *Travels in Alaska* when he died. Coming into being so late in his life, those volumes, eight in all, were perhaps the strings he used to tie together his wandering course.

Self-appointed priest of the Range of Light, Muir had renounced the workaday world for the wider one of nature. In touching the living rock and dipping his head in high mountain pastures, he found real wealth, a wealth he wanted to share. He worked to transform tourists into walkers, to teach humans to see earth as more than simply soil. He believed that the "etiquette of the wild" was not something learned from a book but from experience. The spiritual munificence it gave him could not be diminished, no matter how many years he endured city life or pleaded with its citizenry and politicians to safeguard the wildlands. He let the ice, trees, flowers, soil, storms, and seasons teach him who to be and how to live.

We have only to dip back into Muir's words to find a model for living unconditionally, which means getting on our hands and knees to see, hear, smell, and taste the Earth, and so to daily restore our sense of divinity with the upside-down freshness of all living things. ■

From saving the California redwoods to opposing construction of the controversial Glen Canyon Dam on the Colorado River, David Brower has waged a lifelong struggle to preserve the environment, sometimes working through such organizations as the Sierra Club and Friends of the Earth.

I think people are getting tired of looking at stumps. They're starting to look for beauty. . . . We have to accept the fact that we are trashing the Earth and start asking 'When do we stop?'

~DAVID BROWER

At times the conservation battle has been agonizing, but when my daughter and I ride our horses through one of Muir's 'irrepressibly exuberant' groves, which I helped to protect, my heart is full.

~Carla Cloer

Third grade teacher turned environmental activist, Carla Cloer has become a leading light in the battle to preserve the giant sequoias of the southern Sierra. Her ongoing campaign to save old-growth forests helped create the Giant Sequoia National Monument in April 2000.

The legacy of John Muir lives on in the conservation actions of the generations of people who have been inspired by his work and his words.

~SCOTT HOFFMAN BLACK

As director of the Sierra Nevada Forest Protection Campaign from 1997 to 2000, Scott Hoffman Black was instrumental in saving large tracts of California woodland from the chain saw and bulldozer. He is currently executive director of the Center for Biological Diversity.

Since founding the California Institute of Man in Nature in 1969, John Olmsted has worked to expand and preserve California's parklands, raising money to purchase private property and lobbying legislators for park bills. He is currently trying to create a cross-California trail, from Mendocino to Tahoe.

If, as John Muir said, 'everything is connected to everything else,' then we ought to view our park systems as remnants of the original whole rather than as Indian reservations or islands in a sea of development.

~John Olmsted

JOHN MUIR: NATURE'S VISIONARY

Muir enjoys a moment of silent reflection during a 1907 stroll through Muir Woods, just north of San Francisco.

JOHN MUIR: NATURE'S VISIONARY
by Gretel Ehrlich

Published by the National Geographic Society

John M. Fahey, Jr.	*President and Chief Executive Officer*
Gilbert M. Grosvenor	*Chairman of the Board*
Nina D. Hoffman	*Senior Vice President*

Prepared by the Book Division

William R. Gray	*Vice President and Director*
Charles Kogod	*Assistant Director*
Barbara A. Payne	*Editorial Director and Managing Editor*
Marianne Koszorus	*Design Director*

Staff for this Book

K. M. Kostyal	*Project and Text Editor*
Annie Griffiths Belt	*Illustrations Editor*
Gillian Carol Dean	*Art Director*
Lynn Johnson	*Photographer*
Anne E. Withers	*Researcher*
Carl Mehler	*Director of Maps*
Joseph F. Ochlak	*Map Researcher*
Gregory Ugiansky Martin S. Walz	*Map Production*
Joseph R. Yogerst	*Legend Writer*
Kate Glassner Brainerd	*Designer*
R. Gary Colbert	*Production Director*
Richard S. Wain	*Production Project Manager*
Lewis R. Bassford	*Production Manager*
Sharon Kocsis Berry	*Illustrations Assistant*
Peggy Candore	*Assistant to the Director*
Dale-Marie Herring Robert W. Witt	*Staff Assistants*
Deborah E. Patton	*Indexer*

Manufacturing and Quality Control

George V. White	*Director*
John T. Dunn	*Associate Director*
Vincent P. Ryan	*Manager*
Phillip L. Schlosser	*Financial Analyst*

ADDITIONAL READING

The reader may wish to consult the *National Geographic Index* for related books and articles. The following sources may also be of interest:

Peter Browning, ed., *John Muir in His Own Words*

Stephen Fox, *The American Conservation Movement: John Muir in His Time and Ours*

Terry Gifford, ed., *John Muir: His Life and Letters and Other Writings*

Stephen Holmes, *The Young John Muir*

John Muir, *The Cruise of the Corwin, Letters to a Friend, The Mountains of California, My First Summer in the Sierra, Our National Parks, Steep Trails, Stickeen, The Story of My Boyhood and Youth, A Thousand-Mile Walk to the Gulf, Travels in Alaska,* and *The Yosemite*

Frederick Turner, *Rediscovering America: John Muir in His Time and Ours*

Stephen Whitney, *A Sierra Club Naturalist's Guide to the Sierra Nevada*

Linnie Marsh Wolfe, ed., *John of the Mountains: The Unpublished Journals of John Muir*

Linnie Marsh Wolfe, *Son of the Wilderness: The Life of John Muir*

ABOUT THE AUTHOR

A native Californian, Gretel Ehrlich shares John Muir's love of the raw wilderness. Her award-winning essays in *The Solace of Open Spaces* explore the wide Wyoming landscape and the people she met while living there. In recent years, she has devoted herself to the Inuit of remote northern Greenland, and her experiences with them will appear in an upcoming book. Ehrlich's poetry and fiction have been published in numerous volumes, and her articles have appeared in the *New York Times, Outside, Audubon, Harper's* and *National Geographic Adventure*.

ILLUSTRATIONS CREDITS

ACKNOWLEDGMENTS

OUR THANKS TO Holt-Atherton Special Collections, University of the Pacific Library, and particularly to Daryl Morrison and Janene Ford. We would also like to thank Seth Adams, Save Mount Diablo; David Blackburn, John Muir National Historic Site; Christine Cowles and James Snyder, Yosemite National Park; Frank Helling; Susan Reece, Theodore Roosevelt National Park; and Millie Stanley. We would also like to thank Carolinda E. Averitt and Michele Tussing Callaghan for their careful reading of the book.

The world's largest nonprofit scientific and educational organization, the National Geographic Society was founded in 1888 "for the increase and diffusion of geographic knowledge." Since then it has supported scientific exploration and spread information to its more than nine million members worldwide.

The National Geographic Society educates and inspires millions every day through magazines, books, television programs, videos, maps and atlases, research grants, the National Geography Bee, teacher workshops, and innovative classroom materials.

The Society is supported through membership dues and income from the sale of its educational products. Members receive National Geographic magazine—the Society's official journal—discounts on Society products, and other benefits.

For more information about the National Geographic Society and its educational programs and publications, please call 1-800-NGS-LINE (647-5463), or write to the following address:

National Geographic Society
1145 17th Street N.W.
Washington, D.C. 20036-4688 U.S.A.

Visit the Society's Web site at www.nationalgeographic.com.

Library of Congress Cataloging-in-Publication Data
Ehrlich, Gretel.
    John Muir : nature's visionary / by Gretel Ehrlich
        p.   cm.
      ISBN 0-7922-7976-7 (deluxe) — ISBN 0-7922-7954-9 (regular)
        1. Muir, John 1838-1914. 2. Naturalists—United States—Biography.
   3. Conservationists—United States—Biography. I. Title.

   QH31.M9 E47 2000
   333.7'2'092—dc21   00-060944
   [B]

Composition for this book by the National Geographic Society Book Division. Printed and bound by R.R. Donnelley & Sons, Willard, Ohio. Color separations by NAC, Portage, MI. Dustjacket printed by Miken Inc. Cheektowaga, New York.